27 VIEWS OF CHARLOTTE

27 VIEWS OF CHARLOTTE

The Queen City in Prose & Poetry

Introduction by Jack Claiborne

eno
publishers

27 Views of Charlotte: The Queen City in Prose and Poetry
Introduction by Jack Claiborne
© Eno Publishers, 2014
All rights reserved

Eno Publishers
P.O. Box 158
Hillsborough, North Carolina 27278
www.enopublishers.org

ISBN–13: 978–0–9832475–9–3
ISBN–10: 0–9832475–9–5
Library of Congress Control Number: 2014939796
10 9 8 7 6 5 4 3 2 1

Cover illustration by Daniel Wallace, Chapel Hill, North Carolina
Design and typesetting by Horse & Buggy Press, Durham, North Carolina

Publisher's Acknowledgments

www.ncarts.org

Eno Publishers wishes to acknowledge the generous support of the North Carolina Arts Council's Arts and Audiences grant that helped fund 27 *Views of Charlotte*, and other books in Eno's "27 Views" series.

The publisher also wishes to thank Gita Schonfeld, Caitlin Whalen, Speed Hallman, and Adrienne Fox for their careful editorial work on the views, and Daniel Wallace for his cover illustration.

A huge thank you to our twenty-seven writers and our Introduction writer, Jack Claiborne, who have created a literary montage of Charlotte, present and past.

Acknowledgments & Permissions

Some of the works in this book are adapted from work that appeared in other publications.

A version of Amy Rogers's "A Taste of Equality" appeared in *Hungry for Home: Stories of Food from Across the Carolinas,* first published by Novello Festival Press.

Dannye Romine Powell's story " Fourth Ward in the Gay Nineties" is adapted from an article that appeared in the *Charlotte Observer* on September 14, 1979.

Two of Mary Kratt's previously published poems appear in her view, "The Girls." *The Only Thing I Fear Is a Cow and a Drunken Man* was published by Carolina Wren Press, and *Legacy: The Myers Park Story* was published by the Myers Park Foundation.

Virginia Brown's essay "Roots" first appeared in *Charlotte* magazine in August 2013.

"A Wild Ride" by Peter St. Onge is adapted from a story that originally appeared on May 24, 2009, in the *Charlotte Observer*. It drew on work from the late *Observer* reporter David Poole, and also included editorial contributions from David Scott and Maria David.

Rick Rothacker's essay "When Charlotte Turned Upside Down" is adapted from his story that appeared on September 14, 2013, in the *Charlotte Observer*.

David Radavich's poem "Charlotte Convention" first appeared on "The New Verse News" website.

Anna Jean Mayhew's story "Loraylee" is excerpted from her forthcoming novel *Tomorrow's Bread* and appears here courtesy of Kensington Books.

Table of Contents

Preface

THE QUEEN CITY, Bank Town, the Hornet's Nest, Capital of the New South, Last Capital of the Confederacy, the World Class City, the City of Gold, the NASCAR City, the City of Trees, the City of the Future, the City of Now . . . Charlotte has enough monikers to rival the ancient city of Rome. It is the Carolinas' very own megalopolis and represents many things to its many people. But most would agree that it is vibrant, diverse, and famously synonymous with growth. Just put a native-born Charlottean who's lived elsewhere for a while behind the wheel and ask him to get from Point A to Point B.

To capture such a complex and varied place in 224 pages is as unlikely as a cease-fire in the barbecue wars. Instead, *27 Views of Charlotte* is a literary mosaic assembled by two-and-a-half dozen of the city's novelists, journalists, historians, essayists, and poets writing about some aspect of their hometown. The views span genres, neighborhoods, decades, racial and cultural experiences, generations. Some celebrate the city's victories; others expose its fissures. Some are lighthearted; others wade into troubled waters. Some focus on changing lives in a changing city, on change for the better, but not always.

27 Views of Charlotte is not a guidebook, but a composite of views. Our hope is that the book creates a deeper and richer sense of place, giving readers insight into life in Charlotte today and in the past, and into how twenty-seven of its inhabitants think about the place they call home.

Elizabeth Woodman
Eno Publishers | Spring 2014

Introduction

CHARLOTTE HAS ALWAYS BEEN a pushy place. In naming itself for the British queen who expanded Kew Gardens, established Buckingham Palace, bore fifteen children and raised thirteen to adulthood, the city has had a lot to live up to. For that reason it has striven to catch the next wave in hopes of becoming the first, the biggest, the best, the tallest, the most admired, or whatever other superlative was available.

The marvel is that in becoming the Queen City, Charlotte has often succeeded and has taken every opportunity to celebrate its success. That has won it a reputation for self-promotion. Many years ago a fellow said, "If Charlotte could suck as hard as it can blow, the Atlantic Ocean would be in the Catawba River." More recently a new preacher in town observed, "I've never seen a city so up on itself." Some say that enterprising spirit is in the city's air, others say it's in the water. Whatever the source, it is enduring.

Then there was the former Las Vegas basketball player who, after surveying the town as a rookie professional, complained, "The only thing to do here is live." His lament might have been a put-down, but to many Charlotteans it was more accurate than his jump shot. To them their beautiful, tree-canopied city was essentially a livable place.

Behind the push and swagger have come solid accomplishments. The city has no reason for being—it's not on a river or a bay, has no mountain or other natural feature to give it prominence. It began as a village at the crossing of two Indian paths. But what a village it has become.

The chamber of commerce will tell you Charlotte is a "welcoming, can-do" place that makes big plans and fulfills them. That approximates the assessment of Kentuckian Bill McCoy, a retired political scientist and urbanologist at the University of North Carolina at Charlotte who, after watching the city grow for almost fifty years, attributes its success to the "vision" of its leaders, usually men and women from somewhere else. "Those people came here and made good things happen," he said.

When in the early 1980s, "those people" set their sights on making Charlotte a "world-class city," legions of naysayers guffawed. But after watching the city win an NBA franchise, host men's and women's NCAA Final Four basketball tournaments, lure the North Carolina Dance Theatre, win an NFL franchise that sent a team to the Super Bowl, open impressive art museums, attract the headquarters of eight Fortune 500 companies, become the country's second largest banking and financial center, operate the nation's sixth busiest airport, nurture a 27,000-student research university, operate the state's first light-rail transit system, and host a much-praised Democratic National Convention, the jeers have subsided.

Charlotte is now the sixteenth largest city in the country with a population of nearly 800,000 and growing at a rate of 5.4 percent a year. Former Mayor Patsy Kinsey called it "a big city with a small town feel . . . a quilt of neighborhoods spreading out from the center city," which is itself a neighborhood, housing more than 15,000, many in high-rise elegance.

Two of the city's prized neighborhoods were designed by famous landscape architects—Dilworth by the Olmsted brothers, John and Frederick, and Myers Park by John Nolen. Though now a century old, their curvilinear roads and tree-arched avenues remain city treasures. In the 1910s, when the wealthy were jostling for favorable homesites along winding Queens Road, it was said that Charlotteans believed in "the brotherhood of man and the neighborhood of Myers Park."

Naming the town and many of its streets for the queen has not been the city's only play to power. Over the years its leaders have often sought favors from the privileged, whether political, economic, athletic, or cultural.

In an effort to found the state's first tax-supported college (the tax was on liquor), they named the city's main street for the royal governor, then William Tryon, a man reviled elsewhere in the state, and made him chairman of the school's board of trustees. Though Tryon soon left the state, Tryon Street has remained one of Charlotte's sought-after addresses. Two years later, when the college was up and teaching young Presbyterians, word came that King George III refused to charter "a school for dissenters." Undeterred, Charlotteans renamed the school "Queens Museum," which didn't need a royal charter, and kept on teaching. The school later changed its name to Liberty Hall, moved to Salisbury, and died in the American Revolution. But Charlotte's effort signaled that the city intended to be a significant place.

Charlotteans got even with King George in May 1775 when, learning that British Redcoats had fired on Massachusetts militia, they cut all ties to the Crown by issuing the Mecklenburg Declaration of Independence, one of ninety such petitions rising from colonial communities before the Second Continental Congress brought forth the American Declaration in July 1776.

Unfortunately no pristine copy of the Mecklenburg Declaration has been found, so its legitimacy is roundly challenged. Yet no one doubts the authenticity of the little-known Mecklenburg Resolves, adopted eleven days later to establish an independent local government. Controversy about the Mecklenburg Declaration has hardly inhibited Charlotte's celebrations. Assuming a disputed declaration is better than obscure resolves, they have continued to invite U.S. presidents (Taft, Wilson, Eisenhower, Ford) and other notables (most recently writers Doris Kearns Goodwin and David McCullough) to help celebrate May 20 as "Meck Dec Day." Often all of North Carolina has celebrated with them. The May 20, 1775, date is still a fixture on the state flag and the official state seal.

Playing to power has not always worked to Charlotte's benefit. In 1791 when George Washington passed through on his presidential perusal of Southern states, Charlotteans met him at the South Carolina border, filled him in on local heroics, wined and dined him, and powdered his wig, no doubt hoping to win future favors. They were mortified later to learn that in the diary of his travels Washington dismissed Charlotte as "a trifling place."

All that history helps explain why Charlotte's main crossroads is still known as Independence Square and why the word *independence* is applied to all manner of Charlotte buildings, highways, parks, schools, and businesses—as well as political attitudes. Not for nothing is Charlotte's contentious delegation to the state legislature known for representing "the Great State of Mecklenburg."

The city's early progress was slow until the discovery of gold in 1790. By the 1810s, when deep mining was underway in what is now Uptown Charlotte, a dozen languages were spoken on city streets as miners, chemists, and explosives experts poured in from around the world.

Twenty years later, with help from President Andrew Jackson and United States Speaker of the House James K. Polk, a Mecklenburg native, Charlotte became home to one of the first U.S. mints outside Philadelphia. The Mint brought banking and investing, and made Charlotte a good place to make money. The Mint's superintendents, all appointees of the president of the United States, were men with impressive credentials. Many stayed to increase the city's human capital.

With much of their new wealth, Charlotteans began buying bonds in the South Carolina Railroad in hopes it would build a line into the city. A railroad to Charleston would greatly enhance Charlotte's nascent cotton ginning, baling, and shipping operations. At the time, trustees of the North Carolina Railroad envisioned a line from Morehead City straight across the state to Asheville. But as the South Carolina Railroad inched northward, Tar Heel railroaders could foresee the wealth of the Catawba Valley flowing out the port at Charleston. They bent their route south from Greensboro to meet the South Carolina line at Charlotte. That made Charlotte a wealthy cotton-marketing center until the Civil War.

A glitch in the junction of North Carolina and South Carolina railroads added to Charlotte's distinction. Their rails were laid at different widths, meaning every passenger or shipment passing through had to change trains. Who could forget Charlotte after making that burdensome stop?

After the Civil War, Charlotte's cotton marketing morphed into cotton manufacturing. The city got its first mill in 1881 and by 1900 had a dozen more. With cotton mills flourishing up and down the Piedmont hills, Charlotte became their service center, bringing bankers, lawyers, accountants, engineers, architects, machinists, managers, and salesmen to the city. Since 1880, Charlotte's population has doubled every twenty years — and is expected to double again between 2010 and 2030.

Often Charlotte's reach has exceeded its grasp. In the 1880s, it put up land and money in hopes of becoming home to North Carolina's land-grant college of agriculture and mechanics, but that honor went to Raleigh, where the school became North Carolina State University. In the 1940s as Charlotte was building a teaching hospital, it tried mightily to win the second two years of an expanding University of North Carolina Medical School, but that plum went to Chapel Hill and gave rise to N.C. Memorial Hospital. In the 1960s it was hurriedly raising money to attract the proposed North Carolina School of the Arts only to be outbid by Winston-Salem.

In the gold and cotton years, Charlotte spawned a variety of newspapers, some weekly, some daily, and all short-lived. They generated interest in reading and writing and gave the city a greater sense of itself.

The real expansion of literary interests came with the cotton mills in the 1880s, when the second *Charlotte Observer* was revived as a morning journal and the waspish *Charlotte News* as an evening daily. With Charlotte in both their names and the railroads to distribute their editions, they gave the Piedmont region a greater awareness of Charlotte as a magnet for shopping, entertainment, and employment.

The papers attracted many talented writers, two of whom authored books that became Southern classics. One is *The Mind of the South,* by W.J. Cash, who explored the anomalies of Southern culture. The other is *A Southern Garden,* by Elizabeth Lawrence, known as the "Jane Austen of garden writing." The Queen City continues to draw all kinds of talented writers, twenty-seven of whom are included in *27 Views of Charlotte.*

Over the years Charlotte has sold itself as the City of Gold, City of Railroads, City of Cotton, City of Industry, City of Churches, City of Trees, the Friendly City, and more recently the City of Banking and Finance.

Among the city's many *firsts* are two comical contradictions. In a 1904 wave of indignation, Charlotte became the state's first city to vote itself dry, forcing the closure of sixteen saloons and other liquor dispensaries on January 1, 1905. The rest of North Carolina followed in 1908 by approving statewide prohibition. Seventy years later, after a prolonged struggle in the state legislature, Charlotte became the first city to vote itself wet and began serving liquor by the drink, a privilege since enjoyed by other municipalities in the state.

Legalized liquor opened the door to a wave of new hotels, restaurants, and convention halls, making Charlotte the state's leading visitors' center. It also brought the city a campus of Johnson and Wales University, which has quickened the hospitality industry by training managers for hotels and restaurants, and chefs for haute cuisine.

Once a glowering, after-dark wasteland, Uptown Charlotte now glows with lights and activity as people crowd sidewalks, restaurants, bars, concert halls, theaters, museums, and art galleries under the towering spires of the Carolinas' most dazzling skyline.

Since the 1960s scholars at the University of North Carolina at Charlotte have made the city aware of its history, its environment, and of the teeming metropolitan region around it, warning that continued sprawl breeds problems for everyone. Accordingly, the city has embarked on efforts to grow urban and upward rather than suburban and outward. The challenge is to preserve its easy livability.

The most important quality of Charlotte, however, is not its size or history or wealth or amenities. It is its openness, reflected here in *27 Views of Charlotte.* You don't have to come from a particular family or industry or religion or race to make a place for yourself. If you have ideas and the energy to put them across, you too can be a leader. That's part of what makes Charlotte a pushy and successful place.

Jack Claiborne

Charlotte, North Carolina

JACK CLAIBORNE is a native Charlottean, the author of seven books, and a retired associate editor and columnist for the *Charlotte Observer*. He is the former assistant to the chancellor at the University of North Carolina at Charlotte.

Views from Before

A Capital City

DAVID GOLDFIELD

THE GRITS WERE LUMPY and the eggs tasted like they came out of a box instead of a chicken, but that was beside the point. Three colleagues and I were enduring these culinary crimes for a greater end. We were soliciting the mayor of Charlotte to support our fledgling endeavor, the Museum of the New South. One of our breakfast companions was the executive director of the Valentine Museum in Richmond, Virginia. At the time of our meeting in 1993, the Valentine had earned a national reputation both in terms of the quality of its exhibits and in its service to the community.

The fellow from the Valentine summarized for the mayor the multitude of benefits derived from a city history museum. The mayor sighed and said he understood, but Richmond had a history. The implication, of course, was that Charlotte did not have a history and, therefore, why the need for a history museum. At that moment, any doubts I may have harbored about a history museum for Charlotte vanished.

Did you know, Mr. Mayor, that Charlotte was the last capital of the Confederacy? President Jefferson Davis and his cabinet held their final meeting in Charlotte. They were not in Richmond because Union General Ulysses S. Grant and thousands of Federal troops were occupying that city — making a congenial gathering of top Rebel officials unwise. Charlotte was much safer as the Federals would never think of looking for the absconding Confederate government officials in such an obscure place.

That was probably the thinking of the Confederate authorities when, in May 1862, they established the Confederate Naval Yard in Charlotte. Union forces had destroyed the naval facility at Norfolk, so what better place to hide the Rebels' seaworthy intentions than a place discreetly far from the ocean. Not surprising that the Federals never discovered this brilliant relocation.

Alas, Charlotte's tenure as the capital of the Confederate States of America was brief. Fearing capture, or worse, President Davis and his colleagues went their separate ways. On May 10, 1865, a detachment of Union cavalry seized Davis near Irwinville, Georgia. Word went out that Davis, to avoid detection, was clad in a dress. This was before cross-dressing became popular among public officials. The Northern press ridiculed Davis's costume. In reality, the former president had wrapped himself in his wife's shawl to keep warm. Southern Georgia can get awfully cold in May. But you know how the press exaggerates.

Speaking of exaggeration, rumors circulated that when the cabinet meeting broke up in Charlotte, Jefferson Davis entrusted the Confederate treasury to Judah P. Benjamin, his secretary of state. Benjamin, the story goes, did not want to carry around all that gold, especially after the Republicans raised the possibility that Lincoln's assassination was part of a Jewish plot headed by the Confederate secretary of state. Though this was a Republican fantasy (and not the last), Benjamin took no chances and sailed all the way to England to escape prosecution.

And what of the Confederate treasury? Benjamin allegedly buried it somewhere between Charlotte and Rock Hill, South Carolina, twenty-five miles to the south. Nowadays, anyone who builds a swimming pool in south Charlotte dreams of striking the Confederate treasury. They're wasting their time. Jews don't bury money; we invest it.

As fortune would have it, these two themes, money and religion — usually in that order — would play significant roles in Charlotte's subsequent history. This connection perked up the mayor, because if there is anything that energizes the city's civic leaders it is righteous capital. It is not happenstance that the yellow brick road leading from Charlotte airport to Uptown (we don't call it "Downtown" because we are very Upbeat here) is anointed the Billy Graham Parkway, named for the famous evangelist.

We are also the former home of that Bible-blessed couple, Jim and Tammy Faye Bakker, televangelists who built a Christian entertainment empire. Seldom have money and religion united in such bliss as with this duo. Tammy Faye was fond of saying "You don't have to be dowdy to be a Christian," and she worked very hard to prove her point. Tammy Faye also warned her faithful followers, "You can educate yourself right out of a relationship with God." Trust me, there was never any chance of that fate befalling Tammy Faye.

Jim matched Tammy Faye homily for homily. When criticism mounted about his opulent digs at their Christian theme park, Heritage USA, just outside of Charlotte, Reverend Jim shot back, "Why should I apologize because God throws in crystal chandeliers, mahogany floors, and the best construction in the world?" Clearly, God doesn't like junk.

If you're thinking that tacky Christianity is one of Charlotte's great resources, read Wilton Barnhardt's satirical novel, *Lookaway, Lookaway,* which takes place in the Queen City. A Presbyterian minister confides to his friends that "Christianity in Charlotte possess(es) the aesthetics of the monster truck show at the Coliseum."

All of this is good theater until it intrudes on Charlotte's bottom line. Then the hook comes quickly. One of the primary reasons for our dedication to bringing a city and regional museum to Charlotte was the transformation of the place from a big small town to a budding metropolis.

Aside from the obvious expansion of territory, population, and tax base, this meant diversity. We needed a place to tell Charlotte's story and we needed to connect with the newcomers who had no clue about the city's history (and, as it turned out, some old-timers as well). And what they knew about the South was the Civil War and Bible belt buckles, neither of which resonated with the heterogeneous crowd that has descended upon the Confederacy's last capital since the 1980s.

By the mid-1990s, Charlotte had parlayed its banking industry, which emerged in the 1870s to finance a nascent textile industry, into one of the nation's leading financial centers. Throw in liquor-by-the-drink, Uptown nightlife, restaurants that served more than a meat and three (usually the meat was a mystery, and the three sides were unrecognizable from their provenance), and cultural activities well beyond monster truck rallies. In other words, Charlotte was becoming a real city, and we no longer looked to Atlanta, an ersatz global city strangled by highways, traffic, and crime. Portland, Oregon, was now our role model and, yes, you could get some great coffee and even better light rail in the Queen City.

But this new openness was likely to conflict with the city's religious sensibilities, or at least the evangelical portion of it whose faith could be summarized in a popular bumper sticker: "The Bible Says It, I Believe It, That Settles It." Not exactly an invitation to debate, doubt, dissent, and new information. Even more problematic was the evangelicals' apparent insecurity about their faith, so insecure that they required government intervention either in public policy or in public prayer to support their religious preferences. That worked for most of Charlotte's history, but not by the 1990s. We were still a Southern city by latitude, but by attitude our ambitions stretched well beyond Dixie. Parochialism, no matter how flashy or quaint, could no longer march alongside the city's new ambitions.

The controversy that brought faith and finance into conflict, or at least a certain type of faith, because it was never an issue of God or Mammon, but rather some folks' perceptions of God and their certitude of his position on every aspect of personal and civic life, was the Charlotte Repertory

Theatre's intent to stage Tony Kushner's play, *Angels in America,* in 1997. For religious conservatives mere discussion or presentation of ideas is tantamount to their advocacy. They charged that the play advanced and encouraged homosexuality. For those people who derive their morals, values, and day-to-day operating instructions from television and movies, such confusion is understandable. The rest of us realize that we are not witnessing reality but an artistic representation of it and, in good theater, which this is, it will engage us and give us something to think about.

Fine, the opponents of the play said, but no public money should be allocated to support such a performance. The ringleader of this opposition, Hoyle Martin, a black evangelical Democrat, and the four white Republicans on the Mecklenburg County Board of Commissioners cut $2.5 million funding to the Arts & Science Council, which funded the Charlotte Repertory Theatre. The controversy generated some cringe-inducing quotes in the national media. *The New York Times* claimed the conflict exemplified the "cultural tensions created when a Bible Belt town tried to move quickly into the first rank of American cities." Even the director of the Charlotte Repertory Theatre pleaded with out-of-town commentators that Charlotte "is a progressive city . . . I don't want us portrayed as a hick town or a redneck town." Yet, when a local political leader charged that the theater encouraged "perverted forms of sexuality," it seemed that the outsiders had a more accurate perspective on the episode.

The city's business community, particularly the bankers, had seen enough. If Charlotte wanted to continue to attract the best, the brightest, the most innovative people from around the globe, a rerun of the Scopes Monkey Trial was not the strategy toward those ends. Hugh McColl of NationsBank and Ed Crutchfield of First Union led the effort to restore public funding for the arts and back a "pro-tolerant" slate of candidates for both the county commission and the city council (all of whom won their races). The point was not to banish religion from public discussion, but to place religion where it belonged, as a matter of personal faith rather than as a club of public policy. Only then, McColl believed, could Charlotte return to its "common purpose—make money, build nice things, make it happen." Charlotte had no intention of becoming a "Mayberry with skyscrapers," as the *Washington Post* suggested. The play was staged.

And Charlotte defied the caricatures in the coming years. As if on cue, the year after the *Angels in America* controversy, NationsBank merged with Bank of America and the international headquarters moved from San Francisco to Charlotte. The banking consolidation proved contagious as First Union and Wachovia merged three years later. Charlotte became the second largest banking center in the nation after New York City. Uptown, which was so devoid of cultural and culinary attractions that an ersatz city center was created for the NCAA Final Four in 1994, blossomed into a thriving place not only to work, but also to live and play. Major league basketball and football teams, a burgeoning state university, and a diversifying economy accompanied the transformation.

The journey from Confederate capital to banking capital is a story in itself. It is not the history of Richmond, to be sure, but it is a tale of industry (textiles), migration (black, white, and brown), entrepreneurial innovation, expansion of education, infrastructure improvement, Uptown revitalization, and lots of eager, bright, young people attracted not only by the work, but also by the ethic. Richmond's history did not peak during the Civil War, though its trajectory has been uncertain since that time. For Charlotte, the Civil War was just the beginning. The Confederacy ended here, and the New South began. And the Levine Museum of the New South is doing just fine, thank you.

DAVID GOLDFIELD is the Robert Lee Bailey Professor of History at the University of North Carolina at Charlotte and the author of numerous books, most recently *America Aflame: How the Civil War Created a Nation*, as well as *Still Fighting the Civil War*. He was a founding board member of the Levine Museum of the New South.

Fourth Ward
in the Gay Nineties

DANNYE ROMINE POWELL

ON NEW YEAR'S DAY, 1894, Mr. Samuel Wittkowsky, a Prussian immigrant and a resident of Charlotte's Fourth Ward neighborhood, entertained local banking officials at a two o'clock dinner at his West Trade Street home. When Wittkowsky drew aside the silken curtain, separating the parlor from the dining room, his guests beheld a table set with monogrammed crystal, gold plates, and silver flatware. In the center was a "magnificent" pink lamp, and "forming a canopy over the lamp," according to the next day's *Charlotte Daily Observer,* "were bands of pink satin ribbon, stretched from the chandelier to four points on the table, terminating in large pink bows held in place by gold pins."

And the menu:

Anchovy sandwiches, oysters on the half shell, sherry; bouillon, salmon croquets, little potatoes and celery salad; sweet bread patties, green peas and olives, claret; quail on toast with currant jelly, celery, sauterne; roast turkey, cranberry sauce, potatoes, champagne; asparagus on toast, sauce, salad a la Newberg; English plum pudding on fire, meringue glace, bonbons, fruit, coffee, Roquefort cheese, crackers, liqueurs, cigars.

— *Charlotte Daily Observer*, January 2, 1894

Opulence hallmarked the 1890s, a decade when excess and extravagance stretched, like Wittkowsky's pink satin ribbons, from coast to coast. During this silk-hat-and-plaid-parasol decade, Anna Sewell's novel *Black Beauty* was drenching the country in tears, pianos were multiplying five times as fast as people, and roving organ grinders sauntered into town to churn out "Little Annie Rooney," "The Sidewalks of New York," and "A Bicycle Built for Two."

Despite the money panic of 1893 and the Spanish-American War of 1898, the Gay Nineties' gargantuan appetite for frills and fancies matched Diamond Jim Brady's for food and fashion. San Francisco developed its Nob Hill; Chicago its lakefront; and Charlotte its Fourth Ward, established in 1869 when the city was quartered, strutted to grand-dame status. Bounded by North Tryon, West Trade, Elmwood Cemetery, and the Carolina Central Railroad, the neighborhood became known for its most fashionable houses — curlicued, porch-wrapped, and cupola-topped.

Along a four-block stretch of North Tryon — between Fifth and Ninth — lived many of the city's wealthiest and most influential citizens: R.M. Oates, president of Victor Cotton Mills, Charlotte Cotton Mills, and First National Bank; E.D. Latta, Dilworth developer and president of the Charlotte Consolidated Construction Company (the Four Cs); attorneys Rufus Barringer, Robert Shipp, and Clement Dowd (Dowd was also president of Commercial National Bank, forerunner of today's Bank of America); and physicians Annie Alexander, W.B. Alexander, W.A. Graham, W.H. Wakefield, and W.I. Faison.

Fourth Ward's social activities, with few exceptions, headed the *Charlotte Daily Observer*'s "People Column." Be it "a happy company of little merry-makers" on Mrs. John Wilkes's West Trade Street lawn, high tea at Birdie Burwell's, a progressive whist party at young Herman Dowd's, a watermelon fete at Miss Mary Steele's on Tenth Street, a card party at Algernon and Mamie Reese's on North Church, or a "coming-out party," replete with the "sweet music of an Italian band in the cross hall between the tea room and parlor" at the D.P. Hutchisons on North Tryon, Charlotte was at once interested.

> Society will find itself at Miss Adele Hutchison's tonight, clothed in its most stylish apparel—silks and broadcloth—prepared to enjoy to the fullest her debut party, which promises to be one of the most swell events of the spring season.
> —*Charlotte Daily Observer*, May 22, 1895

Adele's grandfather, E. Nye Hutchison, had lived for many years on a multi-acre estate at the end of North Pine Street. But by the early Nineties, hungry real-estate dealers were slicing the last of the old expansive homesteads into bite-sized, half-acre lots.

When the Overman property at the southwest corner of North Tryon and Fifth, "one of the most valuable pieces of property in the city," was chopped into ten lots in 1893, Samuel Wittkowsky's bid of $85 a foot for the four lots along Tryon, knocking Dr. J.C. Montgomery and E.D. Latta out of the running.

> The sale of the Overman property yesterday created more interest in the realty market than any sale which has occurred here in years. For half an hour before the clock struck 12, the real estate magnates and representative business men began assembling about the court house (northeast corner of Trade and Church). Just as the noon hour was struck, auctioneer H.C. Irwin and Mr. E.T. Cansler, attorney, stepped upon the court house step, and there being no dissent from the question, "Are you ready?" the sale began.
> —*Charlotte Daily Observer*, December 6, 1893

These half-acre lots resold to many of the thousands who flocked to Charlotte, swelling the near 12,000 headcount of 1890 to 18,000 by decade's end. Farmers from the surrounding countryside traded hoes for the high hopes of commerce, and a new wave of immigrants — southern and eastern Europeans — were eager to set up shop in the promised land.

Along with Wittkowsky and Rintel, Fourth Ward boasted such names as Baruch, Hirshberger, Ozment, Schiff, Krueger, Hymen, Lentz, Flaum, and Fasnacht, names that lent a rich rumble to the old-time staccato of McCorkle, McNinch, Henderson, Morrow, Pharr, Berryhill, Graham, Blackwelder, Brady, Latta, Kirkpatrick, Bratton, and Barringer.

This melting-pot commerce provided Charlotte a happy mix of goods. Baruch's dry-goods store on West Trade advertised "Sideboards, China Closets, Parlor Suits and Hat Racks." And its millinery department ("It's like going to Rome and not seeing the Pope not to buy or at least see my millinery") featured wide-hemmed bed sheets for 50 cents to $1.25.

On East Trade, Belk Brothers, billed as the "Cheapest Store on Earth," offered "25 envelopes, 20 marbles, one yard ribbon, 10 lead pencils, two boxes blacking" at its famous one-cent sales.

Charlotte's first five-and-dime, the Bargain Store, between East Fifth and Sixth on North Tryon, "invited the ladies' attention" to "Syllabub churns, 23 cents; tin sugar shakers, 2 cents; wood handle pokers, 4 cents."

Closer to Independence Square, a few stores down from J.N. Hunter's Tidal Wave Saloon and across the street from J.M. Harry's funeral parlor, W.J.T. Robinson boasted, "The only white Barber Shop in the City — Shave 10 cents, Haircut, 20 cents."

And around the corner on West Trade:

> Mr. J.C. Springs yesterday afternoon opened up his barroom opposite the court house. The building was packed — and the sidewalk was a mass of people — all struggling to get inside. The pressure of business necessitated several cashiers and several "tenders."
> — *Charlotte Daily Observer*, April 7, 1892

Charlotte saloons would slosh to a close in 1905, when Charlotte anticipated the 1920 national prohibition, but bicycling pumped a brisk $60 million into the country's economy during the decade. Early in the Nineties, Charlotteans formed a bicycle club, and by 1899 there were seven bicycle dealers in town, advertising the new safety bikes with equal-sized wheels and cushioned rubber tires.

Occasionally, bikers misjudged, as when a speeding North Church Street rider nearly knocked G.S. Krueger's child off the sidewalk. Or when Dr. W.A. Graham loaned his "two-seated tricycle" to two young ladies who careened into the gutter rounding West Seventh onto Tryon.

But bicycling generally prompted merrymaking: relay races to Pineville and Davidson, "picnics on wheels" out Derita Road north of town, and the notorious "club runs" on West Trade.

> It was the prettiest sight of the season to see the men on their silent
> and speedy machines go down the street by twos, and then, at the blow
> of the captain's whistle, understood only to the members, come up
> to four abreast; another blow of the whistle served to reduce them to
> twos again, and then to ones.
> — *Charlotte Daily Observer*, March 30, 1892

Charlotte, too, was pedaling toward a spiffier status in almost every area. By 1896, Charlotte was the junction of five railroads; and by the end of the decade, residents were in "telephonic communication" with Richmond, Philadelphia, and New York.

Early in the decade, a *Charlotte Daily Observer* editorial suggested the sanitary policemen should "prohibit the throwing of watermelon rind, grape hulls and other filth on the streets," and proposed that every merchant "clean off the pavement in front of his store Saturday nights to present a clean appearance on Sunday."

Police Chief J.S. Mason warned that all dogs found on the streets without tags after July 1, 1891, would be shot, and that barbed-wire fences in the city limits would be tolerated only at a penalty of $50 a day. By decade's end, the fine for "spitting on the streets" jumped from $5 to $10.

The Nineties' refurbishing rage included almost everything, from sidewalks to soda fountains to sanctuaries. In 1895, eight carloads of cement curbing arrived for Church Street sidewalks. In 1898, Jordan's Drug Store at the northeast corner of the Square laid out $9,700 for a nine-foot onyx and gold soda fountain, "the handsomest soda fountain between Washington and Atlanta."

St. Peter's Hospital at the southwest corner of Poplar and Sixth, established in 1877 and variously called St. Peter's Home and Hospital and the Charlotte Medical and Surgical Institute, was the site in 1893 of the successful removal of a diseased kidney, the first such operation in the state. By 1898, six months before the construction of a three-story, thirty-unit addition to the hospital, Drs. Misenheimer, Irwin, Gibbon, and Wakefield—with the aid of Dr. Henry Louis Smith's X-ray machine from Davidson—performed another record-breaking operation:

> No surgical operation performed in Charlotte or vicinity ever aroused so much interest as that performed on little Ellen Harris of Harrisburg Saturday at the Charlotte Medical and Surgical Institute, whereby the thimble that had been swallowed by her eight weeks ago, and located by means of the X-rays, was removed.
>
> —*Charlotte Daily Observer*, January 9, 1898

Not everything during the decade went quite that smoothly. Thomas Belk of North Church, who managed the Cotton Oil Company, was relaxing in his hammock and smoking his pipe "with an unusually long stem," one October day in 1891 when he toppled. "The pipe was pressed against the banisters," reported the paper, "and the pipe stem run into his throat, almost cleaving the palate."

And there were the thieves—those "midnight marauders" who bugged the Rufus Barringers on North Tryon until "the general appeared at the bay window with his favorite weapon in hand." Or the thief who yanked all the onions from J.N. Hunter's North Pine Street garden and snatched the eggs from Bryant Overcarsh's West Eighth Street roost. Crime-stopper Overcarsh foxed the thief: "Whenever he (the thief) would take an egg out of the nest, he (Overcarsh) would put a plaster of paris egg in," the *Charlotte Daily Observe* reported. "The hen did not catch on, and neither did a chicken thief who visited his coop Friday night."

Electric streetcars arrived in Charlotte at the decade's opening, and by the time the decade closed, those cars would alter the Fourth Ward's status. The cars began arriving in May of 1891, and slowly replaced the horse-drawn cars in use in the last decade.

> Two of Charlotte's new electric cars arrived yesterday and were unboxed at the powerhouse. They are the same size as the Raleigh cars now being used, but are much handsomer. They are cherry, highly polished and upholstered in green velvet.
>
> —*Charlotte Chronicle,* June 23, 1891

The cars hadn't been on the tracks two weeks when undertaker E.M. Andrews on West Trade bought a new undertaking wagon. It's not "cherry," reported the *Charlotte Daily Observer*, but "handsome" and "upholstered in leather, with silver handles and a dash rail of beveled glass."

One June day in 1891, J.N. Rhyne, a farmer who lived near Mulberry Church, came into town to report a dream he said the cars had prompted.

> He dreamed he left four or five plows at work in a certain part of his field, and when after an absence of an hour, he returned to see about the work, he found that the horses and mules hitched to the plows had disappeared, but the plows were plowing right along all the same and were going much faster and doing better work than when the horses were attached to them.
>
> —*Charlotte Chronicle,* June 13, 1891

Time, like Rhyne's plows, was moving right along in Charlotte, too. Edward Latta, head of Four Cs, built a streetcar track southeast of the city and began developing Dilworth, Charlotte's first suburb. Now architect C.C. Hook began preparing plans for five "new style" residences, which included Queen Anne, colonial, and modern American architecture.

> President Latta, of the 4Cs, has selected a beautiful lot on which to build the handsome residence he contemplates erecting in Dilworth. It is on the right of the boulevard, just opposite the curve at the big tree.
> — *Charlotte Daily Observer*, November 18, 1893

40

"New style" was in, and by the turn of the century, Victorian was out. Fourth Ward would continue until at least the 1920s to be "one of Charlotte's finest," but she no longer reigned as *the* best. By early 1900, the crown passed to Dilworth, and from Dilworth, it would continue to pass to newer neighborhoods.

> One of the most attractive highways now leading out of Charlotte is the New Park Road, extending south from Dilworth. We have several good properties on this fine new road. A very fine suburban building site of about 8 acres, ever near to Dilworth, with cottage, for $1,500. Abbott and Stephens.
> — An advertisement in the *Charlotte Daily Observer*, March 30, 1899

DANNYE ROMINE POWELL has been with the *Charlotte Observer* since 1975, serving in various capacities, including book editor, metro columnist, and feature writer. This story is adapted from an article that appeared in the *Observer* on September 14, 1979. Powell is an award-winning poet with three collections, and she is also the author of the book, *Parting the Curtains: Interviews with Southern Writers*.

My Mother's Eyes

JOYCE & JIM LAVENE

MY MOTHER TOLD ME STORIES of working in the cotton fields when she was a little girl, about five years old. These weren't the smiling-days-of-yore kind of stories. She talked about going with her family, in a horse-drawn wagon, to a Cabarrus County cotton field so big she couldn't see the end of it. In her words, "It seemed to stretch all the way to the end of the blue sky."

Her mother and father, along with her two brothers and an older sister, would pack some beans and rice in a bowl with plenty of fatback, and a biscuit or two. It was hungry work and the food they brought had to last them. They brought water too. It was early fall, and the temperatures could climb into the nineties. Often, there was no shade.

"We'd work from about eight each morning until it got dark and we couldn't see the cotton anymore."

They would go home and fall asleep on wood floors with holes in them, exhausted and burnt by the sun.

For their day's labor, the adults were paid fifty cents, and the children each received a quarter. It seems terrible now to think that people lived this way, but my mother told me she was thrilled to get that money.

"We didn't get to keep all of it, but we got a dime from each quarter. It meant we could buy some candy. Sometimes, I bought a blue ribbon for my hair. It was exciting to have that bit of change."

No one thought about interrupting school for this task, for her brothers or sister. School wasn't as important as making this money that would last to buy odds and ends until other work came along. When the job of picking cotton was finished, my mother and her siblings would go back to the one-room schoolhouse they shared with a dozen other children of all ages.

Each day, my grandmother would get the girls up and put out freshly laundered dresses, hand-stitched from feed sacks, that smelled of Borax and sunshine. They rarely wore shoes, even in the winter. They would take their bowls of beans and rice, along with a handful of sticks or coal they found to help keep the schoolhouse warm.

It was unusual for my mother's brothers to go to school. They spent most days with their father, my grandfather, who was a carpenter. It was more important for them to learn a trade so they could work. They had no thoughts about college.

One of the most exciting moments in my mother's young life was the day a well-to-do bachelor farmer asked her family if they wanted to go into Charlotte with him in his wagon. "There was so much excitement! We each had a little money, at least a few pennies. I was eleven, two years before I got married. I had never been so far from home."

They got up before light and climbed into the back of an old pickup filled with bales of cotton. The farmer was taking his crop to be graded and sold at Latta Arcade, located at 320 South Tryon Street in the heart of downtown Charlotte.

The grading of cotton was an important part of a farmer's life. Cotton was graded for length, uniformity, diameter, and maturity. A farmer's crop made more money if it was graded higher. Cotton brokers would decide as well if the strength, color, and the amount of foreign matter in the cotton would bring a good price on the market.

"You can't imagine what it was like on the day those local cotton farmers brought their crop to market," my mother told me. "They came from all over; Albemarle, Monroe, and Concord. At the time, you might as well have said they were from India and Africa. We were country-folk. We had never seen anything so grand."

My mother and her family marveled at the new buildings and the construction happening on Tryon and Trade streets. So many people had cars, and were dressed in clothing my mother could only catch a glimpse of in the Sears, Roebuck and Company catalog.

The bustling Latta Arcade had an almost holiday atmosphere as farmers sold their cotton bales. They could go out and celebrate another season by purchasing new "city-made" clothes and eating foods they never had at home. The whole family went along—young and old, husbands and wives, teens carefully observing the transactions so that they could one day take over the farming business.

This one day in my mother's memory, with a farmer who didn't have a family to celebrate with him, was the glory moment of her childhood. Not long after that, her family's finances forced her to get a full-time job. She went to work at a restaurant and then used her earnings to buy clothes and food for her family, and a little knickknack shelf for her mother.

While working at the restaurant, she met my father, a sailor on leave. He was from Chicago. At the ripe age of thirteen, she received her parents' consent to marry him. The newlyweds moved to the Midwest to live with my father's family before they finally purchased their own home seven years after I was born.

When I was fifteen, my family moved from Chicago back to North Carolina. My mother's mother was long dead, and her father was dying of cancer. Her brothers and sister were living in Charlotte. Their reunion, after many years apart, was tearful.

One of the first places we visited was Latta Arcade, still on South Tryon Street. It was under renovation. Having grown up in the Windy City, I wasn't very impressed.

I had been raised in a different environment than my mother and was a different kind of fifteen-year-old than she had been. Sure of myself (or so I thought at the time), knowing everything (or so I thought at the time), and headed for college — the first to do so in either my mother's or father's family.

The two-story arcade had a large skylight roof that, amazingly, was still intact. Originally used to create natural light for cotton graders and buyers, it was designed by William H. Peeps, in the Beaux-Arts, neoclassical style. All of which meant very little to me. I was bored and restless. I'd just left behind a real city in the Midwest with my friends and shopping trips for a place and people I barely knew. It was much hotter than it had been in Chicago. I felt like I was melting.

As we stepped into the arcade, my mother stood still, staring at the place with a slight smile on her face. She seemed transfixed by it. What was there to look at? She'd seen bigger, more impressive buildings in Chicago.

That was when she told me this story. I had never known that she was married so young. She didn't plan to even let me date until I was sixteen. I was born when she was fifteen — my age at the time we moved to Charlotte and toured Latta Arcade.

I had never heard about her childhood, the hardships and depravation she'd lived with. Even though we were barely middle class, we were wealthy compared to that.

Suddenly I looked at my mother with new eyes. For the first time, I saw her as someone more than the woman who gave me life. She became more than the woman who made such strict rules for me, who was so careful with money, and who had a passion for grits.

From that point on, I saw her as a woman who'd traveled some tough roads and had managed to survive.

Maybe equally important, I saw her as that little girl with blue, penny ribbons in her wild curly hair, wearing a dress made from a feedbag, her feet callused from running everywhere without shoes, and her blue eyes full of wonder when she first stood looking at this place in Charlotte.

It was a wonder she never lost, as I saw that day she introduced me to Latta Arcade, and we gazed up at it together. That image of her has never faded.

She's gone now, lost to breast cancer at the age of fifty-nine. I've lived many places, but came back to Charlotte to raise three children of my own in this area. I have always been a writer, but finally worked up the nerve to get published. She died the same year my first book came out.

Today restaurants and shops fill the arcade's cotton buyers' offices, and residents and tourists wander through the expansive space. I set one of my mystery novels here and in Brevard Court, the brick courtyard behind the building.

I hope a part of my mother, and her life, is in my work because she's there in my heart every day. I never pass Latta Arcade without imagining a shoeless, little, curly-haired girl smiling at me.

"Life provides the opportunities," I can still hear her say. "It's up to us to take advantage of them, or throw them away."

I'm making the most of mine.

JOYCE AND JIM LAVENE have written and published more than sixty novels for Harlequin, Penguin, and Simon and Schuster, as well as hundreds of nonfiction articles for national and regional publications. They live in rural North Carolina with their family. This essay is dedicated to Joyce Lavene's mother, Joan Blocker Koch.

Factory Whistles

NELLIE, early 1900s

A poem by Mary Kratt

Up here
on the hill farm,
hoeing,
I hear them whistles plain
down
in the far town,
factory whistles
calling.

In our high fields
I've done my share
of killing hogs,
hauling, picking,
plowing, all this
men's work,
now women's too
in a family plumb full
of daughters.

Down there's people
I've not met,
a job that pays,
a new dress, and maybe
a road to somewhere.
I'm 17.
I run away with the hired hand
to keep from plowing.

The Girls

MARY KRATT

BUT WHAT HAPPENED TO NELLIE and her beau? How did they fare down in the factory or mill town?

For a long time, curiosity has led me to the lives of very young girls and women, perhaps because the published accounts were so few. What about these girls who came to cotton mills with their parents, siblings, uncles, aunts, grandparents, lured from hardscrabble Piedmont and mountain farms by handbills passed out or posted at country stores by traveling agents of mill owners? Often storekeepers served also as postmasters inside their stores, where farmers coming for mail or supplies, or daughters coming with them on Saturdays for a peppermint stick, could hear the news. If they could not read, somebody around the store's woodstove could.

Such ads promised regular cash wages, housing, schooling for children, and a better life than harsh, unpredictable farming. Farmers rarely saw cash, and the lure of cotton-mill wages attracted a steady stream of folks from surrounding Carolina Piedmont and mountain farms, enticing whole families to the Charlotte area around 1900.

Into these mills young girls walked, some often tagging along with an older sister to "help," which meant that they worked also. The dexterity of children's small, nimble fingers, especially girls', made them valuable in retying broken threads on the many clattering looms. The widely published photographs by Lewis Hine revealed small girls and boys at work in the South, in and around Charlotte, and in New England in the early 1900s. These photos were intended as a tool for social reform and vividly bolstered a national campaign and legislation to protect children in the workplace.

Since the superintendent forbade Hine from photographing on Charlotte's Atherton Mill property in Dilworth, his pictures and brief descriptions capture young girls near the mills after a shift at work. I have long been fascinated by the faces, clothing, and background captured in these photos. The girls are fair-haired, some with pigtails, showing an earnest, direct gaze. In January 1909, they wear high-button leather shoes covering their ankles, dark knit stockings, plain, solid-color cotton dresses to their knees, long sleeves rolled to their elbows, and aprons, often with a sagging pocket. Some appear to be ten years old or younger. Hine tagged a brief caption to each photo, locating it by date and place, sometimes with a comment such as this: "Hands going home from the Atherton. Little girl came from the mill. I saw others about her size in the mill spinning."

Tobacco tycoon James B. Duke's power plants fed cheap hydroelectricity to mills where a fifty-five-hour workweek was not unusual. Local rail lines hauled bales of raw cotton from nearby farms and cotton gins to mills. Millions of miles of coarse sheeting, shirting, gingham, and plaids came from mills with the names of Chadwick, Elizabeth, Hoskins, Mecklenburg (later named Mercury), Johnston, Savona, Calvine, and Magnolia. In 1904 Charlotte had seventeen mills plus others that operated in nearby Pineville, Davidson, Huntersville, and Cornelius (all on rail lines)—three hundred cotton mills within a hundred-mile radius. In fact, half of the mills and spindles in the South lay within that radius.

Entire families working in the mills lived in close-packed villages tightly circled like chicks around a mother hen. Numerous interviews describe the early workplace as that of a relaxed pace and family-like camaraderie. Because children's work was important to families' income, key elements of childhood were missing. They lacked adequate schooling. In 1913 four months of schooling a year were made compulsory by the North Carolina legislature for children ages eight to twelve. By 1933 North Carolina law limited the daily and weekly hours of children under sixteen, and in 1938 the federal Fair Labor Standards Act put limits on many forms of child labor in America.

49

At the Mercury Mill

HELEN, 1920s

Our three room house
belonged to the mill.
Mother. Four children.
Father had gone.
She worked in the spinning room
at the front of the mill.
We stayed by ourselves
but felt her watching
from the mill window.

We knew not to cross
the railroad tracks or
climb the water tank.
She showed us how to do.
Her boss let her come
at 9:00 and noon and 3:00
long enough to nurse the baby.

For $2.20 a day
her shift was eleven hours.
At nights she cooked
and washed and ironed. Then
she got sick.

I was twelve,
two years too young by law
to work, but the doctor
changed my age on the paper
and I swept floors
at the mill, piles of lint, until
they found out, until
she got well.
I remember that mill.

Mill villages like those surrounding the Mercury, and others in bustling North Charlotte, were filled with small, frame, one-story, mill-owned houses, some with backyards for a garden, cow, and chickens—domestic animals like those owned by many of the families in their former rural lives. On work breaks and rare time off, millworkers made lively, poignant music with fiddle, guitar, harmonica, and banjo. Their songs were often lonesome for the life they left behind.

Way across town, beginning around 1920, the electric streetcar line led to a far different cluster of Charlotte homes in the new, affluent, Boston-planner-designed neighborhood called Myers Park. Here lived many executives of James B. Duke's Southern Power Company whose dams provided water power and electricity to run area factories and cotton mills along the nearby Catawba River and local railroad lines.

Tobacco tycoon Duke, son of a farm family near Durham, who as a teenager delivered wagonloads of tobacco, rose to create the American Tobacco Company with machine-made cigarettes and eye-popping advertising. He brought immense wealth to Charlotte. He bought and tripled the size of a handsome house, adding lawns and fountains. This fine mansion in his power company's "executive compound" at the center of Myers Park was unlike any that Charlotteans or Piedmont Carolinians had ever seen. I interviewed "Dit" Henderson, who recalled girlhood parties with Duke's young daughter, Doris, when the Dukes were in town. Listening to her stories, I glimpsed a world of privilege and wealth that I, as a Charlotte girl growing up on the rural edge of town in the 1950s, had never imagined.

James B. Duke had mansions on Fifth Avenue in New York and in Newport, Rhode Island, as well as an estate in New Jersey. He traveled widely, but he wanted young Doris, his only child, to be exposed to Southern living. When she was in town, she was with her governess and a few selected playmates from the close neighborhood. Dit Henderson told me,

> Everybody liked Doris. Mrs. Duke was gracious. Mr. Duke was charming and good to us little girls. I never realized he was important. He filled nobody's description of the world's richest man. He wore high wing collars, a shiny, rather dilapidated Prince Albert coat, which caused more than one person to mistake him for a waiter or footman.

Once in New York, he was mistaken for a cabdriver. Charlotteans saw him walk for exercise with his chauffeured car following a block behind, and remembered that at dinners he served champagne.

Henderson was among a group of ten or twelve neighbor girls invited to Myers Park parties:

> After a neighbor's luncheon for us, we would go calling on other neighbors, take cards and a card case, wear pale pink feather boas, put on high heels, hats, white gloves. We'd say we were Mrs. Biddle or

Mellon as we introduced ourselves at neighboring houses and had tea. They'd greet you like you were really somebody.

Those who spent the night at the Duke Mansion could ride in the Packard with its mink throw robe. The underground garage had a turntable for cars so they could come out the same direction in which they had entered. And in Doris's room, there stood a harp. Best of all was the grand, welcoming living room, where the little girls watched movies.

Henderson told me how she and other girlfriends got accustomed to the French governess, the butlers in white gloves and coats bringing in trays with fingerbowls and little iced cakes. "And those huge ice cream spoons. We'd watch who was in the lead, then do what they'd do . . . . It was like being in a resort or fancy place when you were in the neighborhood."

In 1924 an historic event took place in the upstairs sunroom of the Duke Mansion, when Duke signed papers to create the Duke Endowment to channel profits from hydroelectric power into life-enriching services for the people of the Carolinas. This act revolutionized Trinity College, a small Methodist school, which as a result became Duke University. The annual gifts from this fund endowed Duke University Medical Center, North and South Carolina hospitals and childcare institutions, rural Methodist churches, and the colleges of Furman, Davidson, and Johnson C. Smith. Such aid allowed Davidson College to survive the Great Depression of the 1930s. Continuing its vision, the Duke Endowment in 2012 alone distributed $120 million in grants to improve health, healthcare, and education in the Carolinas. The total gifts since inception of this endowment have risen to more than $3 billion.

By the time of my girlhood in Charlotte, Duke was legendary and the benefits of his philanthropy and the power-generating dams across the Catawba River were familiar parts of the landscape. Mill villages were beginning to wane. Since I was too young to drive and we lived far beyond the bus line, I never visited Myers Park except to attend an occasional concert at Queens College (now University). I had no knowledge of the area of the Mercury and Highland Park No. 3 mills (later known as NoDa or North Davidson Historic District). Both neighborhoods, on opposite ends of town, became historic districts, listed on the National Register of Historic Places. The elegant Duke Mansion itself is on the National Register. And a large and intriguing sculpture of a young female textile worker with a small boy stands on the southwest corner of Charlotte's central square at Trade and Tryon streets.

The young girls sketched above—the textile workers and the playful Myers Park friends of Doris Duke in the early 1900s—and I, decades later, lived in faraway times and disparate worlds. We knew Charlotte as it was then. Mine was a Studebaker family, and like most other folks who were lucky enough to buy a car, we owned a sturdy one, conservatively colored and dependable because it would have to last a very long time.

Charlotte in the 1940s and 1950s was the kind of town it always had been—no-nonsense and plenty of grit. It respected character, freedom, money, and trees. It was practical and determined. As in its entire history, the city sustained a serious case of contagious ambition. Almost everybody, as I recall, was polite, went to church, and wore a hat. There were so many relatives around I had no choice but to behave.

In those days people came from afar to ride a true novelty, Efirds' amazing escalator; or to weigh themselves on the tall, unique scales at the S&W Cafeteria and toss a penny into its wishing fountain; or to walk through the grand Carnegie Public Library with its high, arching-eyebrow windows. But especially to shop at Belk's or Ivey's. As a girl, my mother rode the train from Gastonia to shop in uptown Charlotte and ride the streetcar for a lark past the high, spraying fountain of Duke's Myers Park mansion. We called the city's center "uptown" simply because it was higher up than the streets around it. You always had to drive or walk uphill to get to the main ridgeline street and shops on Tryon.

Those days before air conditioning and television may have been uncomfortable or a little boring, but nobody talked about it much. An airplane flying over was an event. I did not know then that in my imposing, high-ceilinged Carnegie library uptown, Carson McCullers (sometimes with sherry in her thermos) in the winter of 1937–38 had begun writing the early chapters of what would become one of my favorite books, *The Heart Is a Lonely Hunter.*

As a girl, I knew why roads were called Sardis, Sharon, Carmel, and Providence — those old biblical names leading out from town to those churches. And uptown the streets bore the names of early Scots-Irish settlers: Alexander, Brevard, Caldwell, Graham, McDowell, Polk, and that early royal governor, Tryon. It was mostly a Protestant town where any preacher who had a Scottish brogue was well-beloved no matter what he said. Schools, restaurants, lodging, and water fountains were segregated.

It was a town with few heroes. FDR seemed permanently holy, then Eisenhower, but others were well remembered — Abraham Lincoln, Stonewall Jackson, Robert E. Lee, and, further back, Hezekiah Alexander with his 1774 rock house, Charlotte's oldest. I did not pay much attention to other figures such as Lee Petty, Billy Graham, or the Briarhoppers and their musical radio carryings-on. But my grandmother, who lived with us, had her own heroines in those days, their faces and news about them pasted in her scrapbook: Eleanor Roosevelt, Helen Keller, and Marie Curie.

Girls. My city is named for a girl of seventeen. She was England's Queen Charlotte, chosen from a list of German princesses for marriage to King George III in 1761, the same era when early Carolina settlers cleared forests with axes along the Catawba River, planted crops, and built log houses. In all that time since its colonial village beginnings until now, Charlotte has changed a great deal and not at all. The land enticed spirited settlers during the eras of gold, cotton, machinery, manufacture, education, medicine, communication, airport expansion, and finance. Now its people are immigrants again—whole families moving in, many of them recognizing what natives know—that Charlotte is a good place. The river meanders west of the city through green land glistening with lakes and spires and threaded with highways. The stories I like best are of this place, these people—why we came here, who we are.

MARY KRATT is the author of sixteen published books of poetry and prose, including *New South Women: Twentieth Century Women of Charlotte, North Carolina; Valley; Small Potatoes;* and *Charlotte, North Carolina, A Brief History*. She won the Brockman Campbell Book Award for poetry, the Peace Prize for history, and a North Carolina Arts Council grant. Her maternal ancestors settled in Charlotte's Matthews–Mint Hill area around 1780. Part of this view is adapted from *The Only Thing I Fear Is a Cow and a Drunken Man* and *Legacy: The Myers Park Story*.

A Taste of Equality

AMY ROGERS

IT WAS A LATE WINTER TUESDAY when college student Hattie Ann Frazier and some of her classmates took a break from their schoolwork and went downtown. They stopped at a local Charlotte lunch place, sat down, and looked at the menus. But when it came time to order, the waitresses left their stations, turned their backs on the students, and walked out.

It was February 9, 1960, and Hattie Ann Frazier was black. So were the other well-dressed young men and women who sat on the chrome-backed stools that ran the length of the F.W. Woolworth lunch counter. There would be no food served to those students from Johnson C. Smith University that day.

It had started in Greensboro, just eight days earlier, when four freshmen from North Carolina A&T State University sat down at the whites-only Woolworth lunch counter in that city and politely asked to be served. They were refused. A waitress told them to leave, but they insisted on staying, even after the police arrived. The store manager closed down the lunch counter rather than serve a meal to Franklin McCain, Joseph McNeil, David Richmond, and Ezell Blair Jr.

By February 9, sit-ins were taking place across North Carolina, in Fayetteville, Raleigh, and other communities. On February 12, the movement spread to South Carolina, where a reported one hundred students sat in at Woolworth and McCrory stores in Rock Hill. Through the rest of February and March the movement swept across that state, from the tiny village of Denmark near the Lowcountry, to Orangeburg and Columbia in the Midlands, to Greenville, Upstate.

Back in Charlotte, the movement continued to grow. Just twenty years old, Hattie Ann was one of several hundred protesters in the Queen City who took part in sit-ins that winter. Her parents back home in Lancaster, South Carolina, were worried. "I know I'm doing the right thing," their daughter tried to reassure them. Fellow Johnson C. Smith University students B.B. DeLaine, J. Charles Jones, and Edith Strickland had organized meetings on campus, asking only for volunteers who would adhere to the tenets of nonviolence.

What the black students wanted was the right to sit, be served, and eat as paying customers in the establishments where whites were welcome. And they fought the battle to win that right, not with violent confrontations, but with polite and orderly, yet unrelenting pressure through sit-ins and picket lines. Still, more than a few protests turned ugly. Many students were arrested; some even refused bail, understanding fully that their jail sentences would require them to perform hard labor. This strategy, called "Jail, No Bail," demonstrated the students' resolve.

Then two other Johnson C. Smith University students did the unthinkable. Betty Houchins and Thomas Wright were light-skinned blacks, so light that many people thought they were white. The pair went downtown to Ivey's, a Charlotte department store where the "fine ladies" shopped. The store had a popular restaurant which, like many others, was ringed with picket lines because of its segregation policies. Betty Houchins and Thomas Wright crossed the picket line and approached the roped-off area in front of the store. To their astonishment, the white man who was standing guard opened the entrance and allowed them inside. They quietly made their way to the restaurant, where they ordered chicken salad sandwiches. The waitress was pleasant as she served them. "We were so nervous our hands were shaking," remembered Betty Houchins. The couple paid the bill. Then they went outside and joined the picket line.

As the sit-ins spread from the Carolinas to the rest of the South, the nation couldn't ignore the protests and pickets. Organized bus boycotts had begun in 1955; the March on Washington was still three years in the future. But when African Americans in 1960 united over the right to sit and eat in the presence of whites who were doing the same, the civil rights movement coalesced across the South in a way it hadn't before.

By putting food at the center of the debate, the protesters not only made the issue concrete, they made it universal. Within a matter of months, lunch-counter owners who were losing money, along with civic leaders who had begun to comprehend the protestors' resolve, finally began to relent. By the summer of 1960, the lunch counters started to integrate. But the sit-in movement's leaders considered it only a partial victory since it would take three more years of protests to integrate "white tablecloth" restaurants and other public establishments. In Charlotte, the effort was helped by Mayor Stanford Brookshire, who encouraged white and black businessmen to meet for lunch together.

That Southern society became a sort of civic melting pot in this way opens a window into the region's culture and its cuisine. The events that took place here and elsewhere in the 1960s provide a cultural snapshot of a time and place in the Carolinas, and food was an important component of those events. But neither that time nor that place was unique; the same statement could be made about the 1860s, the 1760s, or almost any other time in history.

I've made my home in Charlotte since the 1990s. In that time I've been interviewing and writing about current and former Carolinians, their experiences, and the traditions they find most meaningful. Among the men and women I've been privileged to learn from are descendants of slaves, colonists, immigrants, and the native first people who lived here long ago. Through times of strife and celebration, of poverty and plenty, food connects us, and our stories comprise a cultural and culinary portrait as complex as any we can imagine.

After graduation from Johnson C. Smith University, activist Betty Houchins moved north and married John Lundy; they made their home in Ohio, where decades later, their children and grandchildren continue to enjoy hearing Betty tell and retell her stories.

Hattie Ann Frazier married Joseph Walker and remained in North Carolina. Many years after Charlotte's first lunch counter sit-in, she still remembered her thirst for "that fountain Coke" she had for so long been denied. "When integration finally happened, we went to Woolworth's and had hot dogs," she recalled. "They looked so good."

And she did one other thing. She took her mother downtown to the Kress store in Charlotte where they had shopped for years. Then, for the first time, they went into the Kress dining room and sat down to eat.

AMY ROGERS is a food and culture writer for National Public Radio station, WFAE, in Charlotte. Her books include *Hungry for Home: Stories of Food from Across the Carolinas.* Her work has appeared in *Cornbread Nation 1: The Best of Southern Food Writing* and *The North Carolina Century: Tar Heels Who Made a Difference, 1900–2000.* She grew up mostly in Michigan and New York, and considers herself Southern by choice.

Street Scenes

A Cup of Grace & Comfort

FANNIE FLONO

ONE DAY, NEARLY THIRTY YEARS AGO, I walked into the Coffee Cup—and fell in love with Charlotte.

It wasn't the food, which was good. No, better than good. It was to-die-for good, in only the way great home cooking can be.

But what won my heart was the tableau of people that squeezed into the 1200-square-foot, cinder-block building that seated only thirty-eight—and the line of people inside and out waiting to be fed. With barely any breathing space between the tables, patrons in grease-stained denims ate their collard greens and fried chicken while nearby pristine-suited business executives ate theirs.

Some of the tables had mixed groups, blacks and whites, men and women. Others were homogenous. The room hummed with conversation, and if you listened closely you could hear the fabric of lives unfold in story after story. Some talked business, others talked football, and others recounted the latest escapade of daughter Sue or son Jeff.

In the South, that kind of intimate comfort between whites and blacks, and the elite and poor, wasn't the norm, even in the early 1980s. To *choose* to almost rub shoulders with people unlike you while eating—one of our most primal activities—was not an accidental enterprise. It was an active decision.

The egalitarianism of it all took me by surprise—and gave me an appreciation that I otherwise didn't have for the buttoned-down city of bankers I had just moved to.

When the Coffee Cup closed in 2007 and was torn down in 2009 to make room for more upscale development, I learned about the history of the eatery that stood barely a five-minute walk from the Bank of America Stadium.

When Withers Turner opened it in 1946, it originally was known simply as Withers Sandwich Shop. It served ten-cent hamburgers and hot dogs, ham and grilled cheese sandwiches for fifteen cents, and T-bone steaks with fries and a salad for $1.25. It later added breakfast. And after so many people simply dropped by for a cup of their good coffee, Withers renamed the restaurant the Coffee Cup.

Withers, who was white, served whites and blacks even then, but blacks were served at the take-out window and sat outside. In the mid-1950s, Withers sold the restaurant to Myrtle Heath, a black woman, who boarded up the take-out window and served both blacks and whites inside—thus making it one of the first integrated restaurants in Charlotte. In 1981, Heath's niece Chris Crawford, a waitress, pooled her savings with another waitress, Mary Lou Maynor, who was white, and together they bought the restaurant. They ran the business together until Maynor died five years later. Crawford then ran it on her own, until she sold it in 1998.

The Coffee Cup's story always felt like a metaphor for Charlotte's race relations. Over the years, there has been a lot of sitting across a table by whites and blacks to work out conflicts and move the city ahead.

Although school desegregation was court-ordered and contentious, some public facilities were desegregated voluntarily. When the city was poised for violence at the height of the civil rights era in the 1960s, white and black business and political leaders joined together to desegregate many restaurants, movie theaters, hotels, and motels. A decade after schools were finally desegregated in the early Seventies, Charlotte would be regarded as a national model for school desegregation. And not long after that, the city would become one of the first predominantly white cities to elect a black mayor.

When the Coffee Cup closed, some bemoaned the symbol that was lost. But just as the restaurant had always been more than the words on its long-standing sign, "Good Food Reasonably Priced," the place itself was much more significant than the issues it had come to represent. People who sat down to eat there learned how much they shared with people who did not look like them or have the same financial standing. They learned not to fear each other—at least not as much.

A few other places in Charlotte have filled the void—somewhat. These days, I find myself having lunch at the cafeteria of the United House of Prayer, a five-minute walk from where the Coffee Cup once stood. The red-brick, two-story sanctuary is a far cry from the humble, cramped quarters of the Cup. There's no shoulder-to-shoulder eating in the House of Prayer's cafeteria, which has nearly twice the seating capacity. And no waitress takes your order at the House. You stand in line, get your own meal, and seat yourself.

Just as at the Cup, however, United House of Prayer brings together a diverse mix of patrons. One day I bumped into the most conservative member of the Charlotte-Mecklenburg Board of Education. Another day, famed civil rights lawyer Julius Chambers was chowing down with his golf buddies. Another day, one of the janitors at my office shouted hello to me from his table.

I was not unfamiliar with the United House of Prayer. In my hometown of Augusta, Georgia, I was introduced to the denomination by my great-aunt, Charity Jones, better known as Aunt Chaney, who was a devotee of this flamboyant Christian faith in which tambourines and dancing play a big part in the church service. Much later I became acquainted with their cafeterias that were open to the public.

It's not surprising these days to see blacks and whites, and blue-collar and white-collar workers eating together. It still says something about Charlotte that many of the city's elite business, political, and social leaders seek out a place where they can share a meal with people from all walks of life, people they might only see in passing otherwise.

One of the reasons I moved to Charlotte in the mid-1980s was because it felt like a city well on its way to becoming what it would become. But back then, it had no professional sports teams. It had few Fortune 500 companies. It had no light rail. It was a city striving mightily to be much more than it was.

A lot has happened in three decades. But I'm cheered when I go to lunch at the United House of Prayer and see the mix of people who stand in line with me. In them, I see Charlotte's past and future, and am reminded of why I fell in love with this city.

FANNIE FLONO is an associate editor of the *Charlotte Observer,* where she has written editorials and columns for more than twenty years. Throughout her career, she has received numerous awards and honors, including a Nieman Fellowship at Harvard University. In 2009 she was inducted into the National Association of Black Journalists Regional Hall of Fame. More recently she was named to the Women's History Hall of Fame at the Levine Museum of the New South. She is the author of *Thriving in the Shadows: The Black Experience in Charlotte and Mecklenburg County.*

A Wild Ride

A Legendary Sportswriter &
the Charlotte Motor Speedway

PETER ST. ONGE

THE STORY BEGINS the way a good stock-car racing story should—
with a duel. This one involves press conferences, two of them on the
same spring day more than fifty years ago. Each is covered by a different
Charlotte newspaper. Each brings news of the first asphalt superspeedway
for our growing region.

One, announced by driver and magazine cover boy Curtis Turner, is
a 1.5–mile oval on N.C. 49 that would seat 45,000 and cost $750,000.
The other, announced by a young dirt-track promoter named Bruton Smith,
is bigger—a two-mile, $2 million track in Pineville that would seat 75,000
and include a football field.

Neither promoter, as it turns out, has the money to build his track. Both
will grudgingly realize they need each other—especially in the year that
follows, when the building of Charlotte's big speedway will endure three
snowstorms, a stubborn slab of granite, and, perhaps not at all surprisingly,

a little gunplay. It is the story of how NASCAR was built here, not with grandeur but by ordinary men with ordinary goals—to make something a little faster, a little bigger, a little more profitable. And all of it comes with one question: How would the late sportswriter David Poole have told it?

David was reporting on this—his next big feature story—in the weeks before he died of a heart attack in April 2009. He was excited about the story behind his hometown speedway's birth and had wanted to tell it for years. After that April though, the story existed only in stacks of notes fetched from his laptop.

There were interviews and timelines, statistics and recollections. The storyteller in David surely would have had some choices to make. Every good story, as he well knew, is an answer to a parade of questions—what quotes to sprinkle in, what details to sift out. And always, the most important to ask: Why tell this story?

The easy answer? David loved history. Sometimes, he would take side trips to Civil War battlefields on his way to and from races at the Poconos. But anyone who read David, or listened to him on radio, or sat within a five-chair radius of him, knew that he rarely settled for the easy answer.

In the first sentence of his first column as the *Observer*'s racing writer in the mid-Nineties, David bluntly informed readers that he didn't like the term "motorsports." NASCAR, he explained, has always been about the people who put those motors in the car, the people who tamed those motors on the track.

He often came back to them in his stories, and some of his finest writing was about them. Maybe that was because he recognized their story most—country kids doing something they loved, chasing an adventure before anyone knew how big the dream could be.

A Tale of Two Builders

So this is how I begin David's story, with people, the two people who built Charlotte Motor Speedway.

One was Bruton Smith, just thirty-two, brash then but not yet the towering figure he would become. He was a tireless worker, one of the best dirt-track promoters of his day. He drove a little himself, before his mom prayed him out of it, but he was no softie — at a stocky five feet ten inches tall, he was unafraid to stand up to the roughneck drivers of the day.

Then there was Curtis Turner — "a movie that was never made," said former Lowe's Motor Speedway President Humpy Wheeler. Handsome, charming, and, some thought, the best driver they'd ever seen, Turner was the Kyle Busch of the 1950s, running full out as often as he could — except back then, remembers Wheeler, the cars couldn't handle that kind of insult. He was also a restless soul, always off on his plane or in his black Cadillac to pursue some venture. Most in the racing business mistakenly thought he was rich.

Turner sometimes ran in dirt races Smith promoted at the Charlotte Fairgrounds before crowds of 1,500 or so. They didn't care much for each other, say people who knew them. Things didn't get cozier when the idea for a Charlotte superspeedway took root.

"I started the whole thing," said Smith, in an interview a few years ago. "You go back to 1956, I talked to Probst Construction in Concord. They wanted to partner with me and build a speedway. I'd already been working on it, but that really lit my fire."

"Curtis was the guy who started on the idea of a speedway on 29 outside the county line," said Max Muhleman, then a writer with the *Charlotte News* and later a sports marketer. "I would go out there with him during the conceptual stages."

Before Charlotte, there were two asphalt superspeedways. Darlington, which opened in 1950, was the first. Daytona, which opened nine years later and could hold more than 40,000 paying fans, brought racing's version of stadium envy—suddenly, everyone had to have one.

As Daytona was readying for its 1959 opening, Smith approached Turner about doing the same in Charlotte. "He said, 'Let's do it,'" Smith later remembered. "Financing? No problem, no problem. With Curtis, anything was no problem when he was talking to you."

But Turner, apparently, had already nodded yes to a group of other partners, including Darlington Speedway's Harold Brasington. On April 22, 1959, Turner held a news conference to announce the Charlotte Motor Speedway—"some stupid track," Smith recently said.

Smith called his own press conference later the same day. His Charlotte International Speedway would be bigger and better, and Smith flashed what he swears now was an architect's rendering of the project. Muhleman thought then that the drawings looked suspiciously like the Daytona Speedway.

Charlotte's media had a good chuckle at the dueling proposals. In that year's difficult economy, building one track was near impossible, let alone two. Smith and Turner knew this, too. Within two months, they decided to work together.

"Curtis was the magnetic CEO type," said Robert Edelstein, the New Jersey–based author of *Full Throttle,* a Turner biography. "He would fly in, give a big smile, bring a bunch of money from some timber deal, and fly back off in search of other possible sources of capital."

Bruton was the de facto chief operating officer, there for the day-to-day details and the grind-it-out fundraising. At one point when money was tight, he drove across the Carolinas, selling stock for the track at $1 per share. He raised $406,000.

On July 29, 1959, the pair broke ground on a patch of land just north of the Mecklenburg County line. It was a speedway that would rival Daytona, they said. Problem was, Daytona had taken more than three years to plan and fifteen months to build. Bruton and Curtis wanted their first race in May 1960, just ten months away.

Remembering the People

About a week before David Poole died, he sat at speedway-area restaurant with three former racing writers—Tom Higgins and Bob Moore of the *Observer* and Bob Myers of the *News*. They were the Mount Rushmore of North Carolina racing journalists; Higgins and Poole together had covered the *Observer*'s NASCAR beat for nearly fifty years.

The gathering was supposed to be a lunchtime thing, but the afternoon slid past three o'clock before the men began to think about pushing away from the table. They talked some about the usual NASCAR topics—best drivers, best races. Mostly, they talked about the people—the good guys and the characters and the tales that would never find their way into a family newspaper. "Those people always fascinated me," said Higgins, "and they did David, too."

Perhaps that's because David remained very much like them—easy to reach, quick to speak his mind, unafraid to offer a peek at his heart. He was, in his columns and radio work, a very intentional bridge between today and the NASCAR he grew up with.

It was a sport often frowned upon in more polite circles in those early years, with brawls in the bleachers often rivaling wrecks on the dirt. "You sure as heck didn't let your kid go to a stock-car race," remembered Wheeler. "It just wasn't the thing to do."

But racing was, if anything, accessible. Mill folks couldn't afford much, but you could go to the junkyard for a '48 Mercury flathead engine and a Lincoln radiator, and if you could weld a decent roll cage, you'd have yourself a race car for $150.

Those cars raised dust at places like the Charlotte Fairgrounds, or Rock Hill Fairgrounds, or Robinwood in Gastonia, where David Poole grew up. It was a time when most anyone could plow a field and have themselves a dirt track. At least two believed they could build themselves a fine asphalt superspeedway in about eight months.

They couldn't, of course.

Charlotte Motor Speedway's first big speed bump showed up quickly, as workers discovered large slabs of granite not far under the soil. As the late, legendary engine builder Smokey Yunick once said, "Bruton and Curtis made a giant mistake. If they'd have searched North Carolina for the worst possible place to build a racetrack, that's where they built it."

Contractor W. Owen Flowe, upon finding the granite, decided on explosives as the solution. Each day at noon, they'd shake some granite up with a blast, often aided with some fertilizer to increase the bang. "We started drawing crowds every day to witness the blast," Smith said. "You'd think a minute after the blast, everything would be fine. About two minutes after the blast, this rock about twice the size of your fist came back down . . . That would have killed somebody."

The blasting caused such delay that by January crews were hired and lights erected for round-the-clock construction shifts. In March, an eleven-inch snowstorm put the brakes on work. Two more snowstorms blew in during the next two weeks. It was, says Edelstein, "almost biblical."

Smith, who was at the track most every day, blamed Turner for some of the delay. "He caused me a lot of problems because I was having to put out fires all the time," Smith said. "He'd be out drinking, and he'd hire somebody to come and work at the speedway. They'd show up and I'd have to explain to them, you don't have a job and please go away."

Said Edelstein of Turner, who died in a plane crash in 1970, "Curtis may have been, at times, an absentee father of the speedway, but I don't think he loved anyone or anything more in his entire life. And he did work on it."

The delays contributed to an already swollen bottom line—close to $2 million in costs instead of the planned $750,000.

That's what led to the gunplay.

Let's go to David Poole's notes:

> Contractor W. Owen Flowe, in an effort to collect money he believes
> he is owed, orders his crews to halt work immediately. He places bull-
> dozers and earth-movers on the last short strip of the track surface that

remained unpaved and his operators stay on their machines, refusing to move. Turner and Smith brandish weapons and force the machine operators to leave. The bulldozers are hot-wired and moved out of the way, and the paving is completed.

Did it happen?

Smith said no. Well, sort of no. Turner did have a shotgun, he remembered. "He went over there, acting like he was somebody. A guard went up to him and took it away from him."

The Charlotte Observer reported it a bit differently on June 10, 1960, quoting Flowe as saying Turner, Smith, and a group of men held guns on his watchmen. "I told my men to go on home and not get killed," Flowe said to the *Observer*.

The men left the track, and the paving was completed.

Smith years later would say, "I thought it was really great."

The Race

A moment for contradiction, please.

What drove David Poole most batty on his beat—NASCAR's situational governing, the molding of rules to the moment—is part of what charmed him about racing's early days. Haphazardness, as much as NASCAR tries to avoid it now, is the trait that links it most to its past.

That might never be more true than with Charlotte's first race. Scheduled for Memorial Day 1960, the World 600 was postponed until June 19 because of construction delays. Even that wasn't enough time for the proper curing of the asphalt, which was poured only about a month before the new race date. At the first race practice, on June 15, it was clear that everyone was in for an adventure.

"Four gravel-deep holes grew out of the asphalt in the groove on the second turn," wrote the *Observer*'s George Cunningham, who added,

"Practically the entire surface on the third and fourth turns resembled an old lady's wrinkled face."

On Race Thursday, June 16, Fireball Roberts took the pole with a speed of 133.904 mph, and drivers fretted about the cratering pavement beneath them. "The people want blood and I'm afraid we'll give it to them," said "Tiger" Tom Pistone.

On Race Saturday, June 18, drivers were told they could install wire screens over the grills to protect radiators from the inevitability of flying pavement.

Finally, on Race Day, workers hustled to put up the final 400 feet of fence on the back of the track. Bruton Smith wished for the 600 to last at least 300, so he wouldn't have to give customers their money back. Also, he remembered, "I really wanted it to be something."

It was. Tires blew frequently in the sixty-car field. Fireball Roberts spun out twice. Junior Johnson tore up the homestretch fence. "I'd say there was a chunk of asphalt that weighed five to ten pounds that hit my windshield," Johnson later recalled. "Nobody knew if they'd run the race to the end."

Jack Smith led much of the race in his 1960 Pontiac, but his five-lap lead was erased when a chunk of track put an irreparable hole in his gas tank. Joe Lee Johnson, a thirty-year-old mechanic who lived most of his life in Spartanburg, took over first for his only superspeedway win in a seven-year career. He collected $27,330.

"There were some mangled automobiles, some snorting drivers, some tears, but no blood," wrote the *Observer*'s Herman Helms. "Miraculously, there was no blood."

There were, however, 20,000 cars, an estimated 60,000 fans, all going to the same place. "No one had seen anything like it," Wheeler remembered years later. The story of Charlotte Motor Speedway had begun, and the story of racing was changing.

Bruton Smith would lose control of the track, then eventually get it back. Curtis Turner would get voted off the speedway's board and get kicked out of NASCAR for trying to form a union. The track itself would get saved in the 1960s by investor Richard Howard, then endure the thin years of the 1970s, then come roaring back as Lowe's Motor Speedway. David Poole would graduate from the University of North Carolina at Chapel Hill, get his first newspaper job in Gastonia, then eventually come to Charlotte, where he spent twelve loud years as the *Observer's* racing voice.

A few weeks before he died, David called Rob Edelstein about Charlotte Motor Speedway. Edelstein considered David a mentor, and they shared a mutual worry about NASCAR—that in the sport's perpetual search for growth, something important was getting lost. NASCAR, David believed, always was and always should be about regular folks driving cars fast—and regular folks watching them.

"For them," David once wrote, "racing is one of their celebrations of life."

And so he began to report the story of Charlotte Motor Speedway, because the beginning matters, and maybe because it was the beginning of his story, too.

One Thursday, nearly fifty years after the first big race and three days before what would have been David's next one, track officials and journalists gathered in the infield media center at the speedway. There, they unveiled two plaques, including a gold-plated rectangle above the entrance. *David Poole Deadline Media Center,* it read, now attached to his hometown speedway, now a part of its tale.

PETER ST. ONGE is an associate editor for the editorial pages of the *Charlotte Observer.* He's worked at the *Observer* since 1999, and he's won national awards for storytelling in news, sports, features, investigations, and business. He lives in Charlotte with his wife and two sons, who like baseball. But one of those sons wears No. 24 on his uniform.

Charlotte Convention

DAVID RADAVICH

I don't know where
you will find much history.

In museums,
in roped-off displays
and a few park-like estates
with docents and maps.

The real time
is only now

and we are living it
without shadow

like a 2-D
group of faces

trying to be upbeat,
trying to be hip
and young and beautiful.

And we are

full of blood now
with few memories,

but you'll notice many
pleasant streets

that curl
and rename themselves

with willow oaks
as sentinels

and only the civil war
that race remains

and class extremes
dividing neighborhoods
with an elected fence.

Somehow we were hornets*
at the beginning

and we're still
swarming

now and in the day
of our becoming.

*British General Charles Cornwallis described Charlotte as a "hornet's nest of rebellion"
during the Revolutionary War.

DAVID RADAVICH's books include *America Bound: An Epic for Our Time*; *Canonicals: Love's Hours*; and *Middle-East Mezze*. His latest collection is entitled *The Countries We Live In*. His plays have been produced across the United States, including six Off-Off-Broadway, and in Europe. He has served as president of the Charlotte Writers' Club and vice president of the North Carolina Poetry Society.

Charlotte Noir

CATHY PICKENS

CRIME CASES MAY BE an unusual perspective from which to view a city, but I'm a mystery writer, so I won't apologize for that quirk. In years of traveling, I've found crime an interesting perspective from which to view any place and its residents, their history, the things they fear, the ways we're the same, the ways we differ. Our crimes and how we view them define us, like it or not.

On a night tour of the underground tunnels in Edinburgh, Scotland, a costumed guide made real a Black Death and desperate crimes that haunted those stone streets; reading a book by a local forensic scientist while visiting South Africa gave me a clearer understanding of apartheid than any number of histories could have; following a Chapel Hill–trained historian, his white suit cigarette-stained, a drink in one hand and a cane in his other, through the French Quarter, gave a glimpse of Louisiana scandal through a New Orleans native's window: Those stories and others helped me understand.

So what of Charlotte? In a modern city of gleaming buildings, knotted interstate highways, and exploding suburbs, can crime really be a window to understanding such a place?

When I moved from South Carolina hill country in the early 1980s, my father was less than thrilled to have his eldest chick head to the big city— a city he knew for its motorcycle gangs and professional wrestling. Not too many years before I arrived, those motorcycle gangs figured in the first Charlotte crime story to attract my attention.

Biker Gangs

Harry Hoover, now a friend of mine, was the first reporter on the scene in July 1979. The first body was sitting on the front porch, propped back in a chair with a handgun in his lap, looking as though he was napping on a hot summer day. Inside the house, a sixteen-year-old girl was one of the other four victims. Bridgette "Midget" Benfield's family had worried about her hanging out with the Outlaw biker gang, a rough life for any woman, but especially one so young.

In those days, plenty of suspects could be found among the biker sub-culture; Charlotte was home to both the Outlaws and Hells Angels. Rival gang score settled? Internal squabble? Maybe the rest of us wouldn't have cared much what bikers did among themselves, until we saw the news-paper photo of a smiling girl named Midget. The crime remains unsolved, an anomaly in Charlotte, which typically solves homicides at better than the national rates (76 percent is Charlotte's average in recent years, compared to the 65 percent national average). New people arrive, memories fade. The newspaper no longer runs anniversary articles with Midget's picture.

Sex, Lies, and Hubris

With NationsBank's acquisition of California-based Bank of America in 1998, Charlotte became the second-largest financial center in the U.S. Before that, Charlotte was the center of a financial empire of another kind—a unique mixture of money and religion, hubris, sex, and scandal: Jim and Tammy Bakker's PTL Club. What started as a religious talk show grew into a religion-themed broadcast network, then a 2500-acre theme park with a timeshare high-rise and residential lots. The Bakkers attracted followers who sought a family-friendly, faith-filled haven. In the mid-1980s, they raised $158 million but siphoned off so much for lavish living, they couldn't build the vacation rentals they'd sold.

Jim and Tammy started their evangelical PTL ministry (Praise the Lord, or People That Love) in Charlotte in 1974. By the time I moved to Charlotte, rumor and jokes about the over-the-top goings-on at the "Pass the Loot" Club were supplemented by Pulitzer Prize–winning coverage by *Charlotte Observer* journalist Charles Shepard.

Conspicuous consumption on that level is hard to hide in your hometown. A preacher in a sex scandal is even harder to ignore.

Fifteen years after beginning to build an empire, Jim resigned at the center of a sex and financial fraud scandal and was led away with his jacket hiding the handcuffs, his face distorted with grief and tears, a small man given a huge forty-five-year criminal sentence (later reduced).

Many tuned into the unfolding saga because, after all, these were TV personalities and they talked to whoever would listen, from *Larry King Live* to the national news outlets. Listeners enjoyed explanations from the chatty, overly made-up Tammy and diminutive Jim, rumors of homosexual sex-capades, criminal allegations of drugging and raping a church secretary, millions of dollars diverted from religious fundraising to buy gold-plated bathroom fixtures and an air-conditioned doghouse, and conspiracy theories born of the devil.

Amidst that, though, were those who'd been believers. They never got much airtime. They were sad and embarrassed, for themselves and for those they'd believed in. They'd sent their $20 contributions from their Social Security checks or bought into the over-sold timeshares looking for a wholesome Christian place to vacation with their grandchildren. Some moved from other parts of the country to live in the vast resort full-time. Then it all collapsed in an embarrassing, sordid heap.

What likely started for the Bakkers as a genuine ministry of faith ended up illustrating the end for all sorts of leaders who surround themselves with the wrong people, who are too successful, who become too godlike or fly too close to the sun, and who ultimately fall to earth. What better cautionary tale at the intersection of Charlotte's deep religious roots and its financial high-flying.

Kim Thomas

Why do some cases attract the public's attention and others seem to slide by on the periphery? Say the name *Kim Thomas* or show the now-familiar headshot of a cute brunette who, though frozen in black-and-white newsprint, would be described as "vivacious." Anyone who's been in Charlotte since 1990 will recognize her or her name: the young mother, wife of Dr. Ed Friedland, a Charlotte kidney specialist, their adopted ten-month-old crying, alone in his crib all day, while his murdered mother lay down the hall in the master bedroom. She had run to escape the intruder who stabbed her twenty times.

Or was it her husband she was running to escape? Was that the part of the story that captured our attention? Or that they lived in the lovely Cotswold neighborhood and were young and were putting together the life that should be dream material, not end as a nightmare?

Nightmare it was and remained. In 1990, a petty criminal and neighborhood handyman, Marion Gales, was an initial suspect, but attention moved to Dr. Friedland early on. Police got a tip about his extramarital affair. The marriage wasn't going well. He could be a bit prickly. Later, rumors were that the crime scene seemed too clean and orderly, unlike Gales's usual break-ins, and the murder showed too much rage, seemed too personal.

The charges against Friedland were dropped when a judge ruled prosecution evidence on time of death inadmissible; that testimony came from an O.J. Simpson star witness, Michael Baden, former New York City medical examiner.

Rather than fade into the background, Friedland did the unusual: He sued handyman Marion Gales in civil court. The civil jury decided Gales killed Kim Thomas and ordered him to pay Friedland $8.6 million, though no one is waiting on that payday. Of course, indigent Gales didn't have money to present much of a case for his innocence. So the trial and the verdict left even more questions, and people viewing from the outside wondered what didn't get said.

Friedland also tried to sue the city of Charlotte and four police officers for malicious prosecution, but the judge dismissed that case, saying the police had enough evidence to charge him at the time. Defending itself cost the city a reported $4 million.

Gales was later sent to prison for a similar crime, the murder of a woman in her home. That left more questions.

The pain of not knowing, on both sides, has kept the story alive. A tree commemorating Kim Thomas grows in Freedom Park. For Charlotte, she represents the heartbreak of any family with an unanswered loss and lots of questions—and a view of our own vulnerability where we think we're safe.

The Unexpected Serial Killer

Little-known outside Charlotte is its own extranormal serial killer—unusual because of who he was and because of who he killed. Henry Louis Wallace was black. He preyed on his friends and acquaintances. According to the FBI Behavioral Science Unit (the profilers made famous by one-time Charlotte reporter-turned-novelist Patricia Cornwell), neither of those was supposed to be the norm.

Was that why no one really noticed? Some argued that black women are so marginalized that no one cared. But plenty of people cared. Michelle Stinson's sister was three when Michelle died. Twenty years after the murder, she commented on a YouTube video memorial, saying how much she missed getting to know her sister. The most-reprinted photo of her sister shows Michelle bending over, maybe taking a sip of something? A young woman, like the others, living her life. Most of the nine Charlotte victims were single moms, most of them worked in fast-food restaurants or retail. Some were attending Central Piedmont Community College or were working to make better opportunities for their children. All of them lived around Eastland Mall.

Unfortunately for them, they all crossed paths with a charming, young black man who seemed to love women and babies, and was even called "Uncle Henry."

Why did no one notice a pattern sooner? That's the question that's always asked in such cases. He operated for twenty-two months, from 1992 to 1994, when Charlotte's annual murder rate was eighty-seven among a fast-growing population of 400,000. (To compare, Charlotte saw fifty-two murders in 2012 and had more than double the population.) Twenty years ago, the police had only seven full-time investigators. Could they have put the pieces together faster? Or was Wallace that good?

The murders all took place in a five-mile radius in east Charlotte. The community was scared, pushing for action, blaming the police for not doing more or for ignoring the cases because the victims were black women. Those cries had to be painful for lead investigator Detective Sergeant Gary McFadden, who was black.

This killer cleaned up the scenes. This killer had extraordinary access to the women he killed. He eluded police dragnets. He defied the rulebooks given to serial-killer hunters. In the end, though, it was good detective work that found him. Too many of the women had one common name somewhere in their lives: the friend of a sister, a customer in a Taco Bell, the friend of an ex-girlfriend. Too many connections.

Unfortunately for his last victims, he seemed either to increasingly enjoy the killing or to need more money for drugs in the final days. He killed three in the last three days before his arrest.

Henry Louis Wallace as the "Charlotte Strangler" hasn't achieved the notoriety of Wayne Williams, convicted of the Atlanta child murders, or Derrick Todd Lee, the Baton Rouge serial killer. Charlotte's civic promoters, always wondering why the city gets overlooked, are likely glad its serial killer is ignored. The victims' families and those touched by their loss continue to make sure the women aren't forgotten.

The Big Heist

Charlotte likes to consider itself sensible, serious, all grown up, but it couldn't pretend the infamous Loomis Fargo heist didn't happen here just because the gang came from across the Catawba River in Gaston County.

At $17.3 million, it wasn't the biggest theft Loomis Fargo suffered in 1997. It was the most publicized, though. Tall, skinny employee David Ghantt was videotaped for an hour at the Loomis facility, loading cart after cart of cash, rolling it out the door. Cash in small denominations is amazingly bulky and heavy, Ghantt and friends discovered, so they abandoned over $3 million in a Loomis van in the woods.

Ghantt disappeared. The FBI quickly connected him to a girlfriend, Kelly Campbell, and through her to the likely mastermind—tall, husky Steve Chambers, the only one of the group with a criminal record. Phone taps revealed Ghantt had fled to Mexico. After a few months, his M&M'S and comic book expenses had eaten into the small amount of cash he'd taken with him and he was anxious for delivery of his share of the loot.

The gang was planning to deliver a hitman instead, to eliminate the only identifiable connection with the crime. Unfortunately for them, they'd all become identifiable. A note for would-be bank robbers: Take the money and leave your hometown. Moving from your mobile home into a $635,000 country club house attracts attention, especially if you pay cash. So does paying for a minivan in $20 bills and asking bank tellers how much money you can deposit without filling out government paperwork.

Because no one was hurt, we could laugh about the plan hatched while drinking beer at a cookout. They eventually brought in friends and family (twenty-four people were convicted) — hiding that amount of cash is more cumbersome than one might think. And they were generous: Among their more celebrated purchases were breast implants (more than one set) and an Elvis-on-velvet painting. Not to let truth interfere with a good story, but truth is, the velvet Elvis was already in the country club house when the Chambers moved in, a house-warming gag gift left behind by the previous owners.

No matter its true provenance, Elvis-on-velvet was listed among the property seized and was eventually auctioned off to Tom Shaw of American Gun & Pawn Shop for $1600. The blue plastic barrel where they hid some money sold for $1050 to a Charlotte recycler.

The conspirators mostly pled guilty, served their time (five and a half years for Ghantt; seven and a half for Steve Chambers; seven years for lawyer Jeff Guller, angry about being tried for holding a briefcase with $433,000, saying other lawyers had done worse and not been punished). They've tried to resume their lives under the radar. Ghantt, in a prison interview, said he wasn't going to apologize. In his job, he'd worked too hard for too little money, and his five months on the lam were "the most exciting time of his life." They seemed to know they wouldn't really get away with it, but still they decided to "take the money and run" — the name of the song playing on the radio as Ghantt drove his truck to work that day.

Fame & Fortune

Rae Carruth was first known in Charlotte as 1997's twenty-seventh NFL draft pick, with a four-year, $3.7 million contract to play wide receiver for the Carolina Panthers. Football fans expected great things—until he brought Court TV and star forensic expert witness Henry Lee (also of O.J. Simpson fame) to town and introduced us to a lethally amoral, articulate behemoth named Van Brett Watkins. Watkins's rap sheet was long but of no consequence to most of us, the way of most petty criminals on the fringe. Only when he became the hired hitman for an NFL receiver did we pay him any attention.

In 2013, as I write this, road crews are busily widening Rea Road between Colony and Highway 51. I still can't drive into what was once a tree-lined, secluded little dip in a two-lane road without thinking about Cherica Adams driving that same stretch, leaving the late-show movie she'd watched with her boyfriend, Rae. In 1999, the part-time realtor and one-time men's club dancer was sitting sassy in her BMW. Rae led the way in his Expedition down the dark section of road. He stopped, her car behind his, to let another car pull alongside her. Six shots punctured her car door and shattered her window.

Anyone who has heard what happened next, even without knowing Cherica, knows she had to be feisty and strong. Hit four times, she managed to turn right into a small subdivision, into the yard of the first house. She honked her car horn and summoned the homeowner. She called 911 and, in a shaky voice, told the dispatcher what had happened and who was involved. She even wrote out a note when she got to the ER, prompted by the physician trained, as many in Charlotte are, to preserve evidence. Doctors saved her baby. She hung on for a month before she died. The police went looking for Rae Carruth and found him in Virginia, hiding in a car trunk.

This tragedy embarrassed Charlotte. Jerry Richardson, the owner of the relatively young Carolina Panthers franchise, the only NFL owner to have played in the league, was known to hire for good character. This wasn't the kind of player or the kind of publicity he wanted—or that anyone wanted for him.

Watkins, the guy who admitted pulling the trigger, pled guilty, got life, and helped put Carruth in prison, in one of the most riveting performances I've ever seen on a witness stand. Court TV later featured his testimony among its most memorable courtroom moments.

The real heart of the case, though, is Chancellor Lee Adams, the little boy Cherica fought to save—the little boy Rae wanted to kill so he wouldn't have to support him. Cherica's mother, Saundra Adams, is raising him. Because of Cherica's blood loss, his brain was damaged. He's got cerebral palsy and requires a lot of care. But a happier thirteen-year-old would be hard to find, a loving spirit that infects those who meet him, including a *Sports Illustrated* writer whose article made me cry.

Saundra Adams gives us another important picture of Charlotte: a woman of faith deep enough to offer forgiveness. Van Brett Watkins has written her from prison; he's sent $5 or $10 at times to help her out; he asked her to forgive him. In a beautiful note, she acknowledged the hole in her heart, but she prayed he would have peace.

A loving teenager who looks startlingly much like his self-absorbed father, and a grandmother with a hole in her heart—those pictures of resurrection from the worst of indifference and evil are the other side of the worst that people can do.

Razor Girl

I first learned of Razor Girl's 1926 case visiting a Charlotte-Mecklenburg Police exhibit at the Charlotte Museum of History in 2010. No historical crime review of a Southern city can overlook a case that so neatly highlighted the privilege of being a murderess in an older South—at least if you were small and funny and knew how to flirt.

True, her twenty-three-year-old bigamist husband, Alton Freeman, was, as we say, no better than he ought to be. A convicted thief, he'd been running around on her, living off her $15-a-week factory wages. One night, he told nineteen-year-old Nellie he was leaving her as soon as he pulled off a whiskey heist.

Nellie calmly told the officer who later arrived at their little house that she'd hugged him around the neck, asking if he didn't love her. He didn't. She didn't know how sharp the knife was, she said, until he lay on the floor, only a bit of flesh and bone holding his head to his body.

Nellie wasn't shy about talking to police and to newspapers. She attracted the best lawyers in town to her defense team. Until then, Charlotte juries had a habit of acquitting women of murder, and prosecutor and former mayor Frank McNinch vowed he'd see the end of women getting away with murder. The battle was set.

The courtroom was packed every day of the trial. Women in particular flocked to see the spectacle. After all, a woman couldn't be sent to prison, could she? That wasn't the done thing. On the courthouse steps, the only thing missing was a cotton candy vendor, but someone was selling replica straight razors to commemorate the event.

The jury deliberated for two days, read some Bible verses on forgiveness, talked the manslaughter hold-outs around, and found Nellie Freeman not guilty by reason of insanity, it being not unheard of that a woman could be "struck crazy" for a short period of time, long enough to kill a lying, cheating husband. The judge allowed her to take her bloodied dress and razor with her, and she seems to have vanished from Charlotte.

Closer to Home

Crimes help define us, as Jack the Ripper gives us a window on 1880s London. Would Jack the Ripper have been as mesmerizing if we'd ever gotten to see his face? He's been imagined as a member of the royal family or a famous painter or an elegant but crazed physician skilled with a knife — or an ordinary butcher skilled with a knife.

What if we'd ever gotten to glimpse that face, put a name to him? Would he have still been so scary? So capable of luring us with his horror? Or would he have suddenly seemed . . . manageable? Somebody too much like the rest of us. Like kindly Henry Wallace or successful Rae Carruth or flirty Nellie Freeman. Would his victims have been, at the same time, that much more heartbreaking, closer to home?

In the faces we get to glimpse, I see Charlotte's story as a mix of sex, race, money, growth, greed, strong families, deep faith genuine and subverted, a longing for national recognition, and a pretty good sense of humor about ourselves. Not a bad picture.

CATHY PICKENS is the author of *Southern Fried, Done Gone Wrong,* and other books in her award-winning Southern Fried Mysteries series, as well as the walking tour, *Charleston Mysteries.* She writes a column on crime histories for *Mystery Readers Journal.* As herself, Cathy Anderson is a professor teaching law and creativity at the McColl School of Business at Queens University of Charlotte. She is a founding member of the region's Forensic Medicine Board which trains physicians, nurses, and others on preserving crime evidence.

When Charlotte
Turned Upside Down

RICK ROTHACKER

IT WAS A STRANGE TIME in Charlotte, where normal life — commutes to work, trips to the grocery store, Panthers games — ran on a parallel track to earth-shattering eleventh-hour deals, weekend government rescues, and stomach-turning plunges in the Dow Jones industrial average.

The raging financial crisis six years ago would change this city and its big banks — Wachovia and Bank of America — forever.

During the weekend of September 13 and 14, 2008, as a *Charlotte Observer* banking reporter, I worked the phones at my desk while banking executives gathered at the Federal Reserve Bank of New York to hash out the fate of the tottering Lehman Brothers investment bank.

A source that Saturday told me he wouldn't be surprised if Bank of America passed up its chance to buy Lehman to instead nab Merrill Lynch — a bold move in keeping with the bank's penchant to buy up rivals at their most desperate moments. Later, on Sunday, word leaked that, indeed, Bank of America had a $50 billion deal to buy Merrill Lynch, and that Lehman Brothers would file for bankruptcy, spinning the financial system into chaos.

By Wednesday, I was in New York to cover the story of Bank of America's latest blockbuster. There I found even more surreal moments. A luxury car show was underway at the Merrill Lynch headquarters, even as the Wall Street icon was turning to Bank of America for a lifeline. One employee told me that as he walked to work that morning a construction worker at the nearby World Trade Center site called out, "Good luck, guys."

Of course, much more was to come.

In the next two weeks, Wachovia bank found itself in a deal to be sold to Citigroup—only to have Wells Fargo swoop in with a better offer. In a reaction never to be expected in Charlotte—where banks were always buyers, never sellers—Wachovia employees celebrated when healthier Wells Fargo agreed to acquire their bank, rather than Citi, which seemed on life-support itself.

For me and my colleagues, sleep was hard to come by as we scrambled to cover the ever-changing story. During a brief respite at home, I remember falling asleep during a playoff baseball game between my Philadelphia Phillies and the Milwaukee Brewers. At least the Phillies went on to win the World Series.

Just as in sports, winners and losers have emerged from the financial crisis. And there are those stinging what-if moments that will haunt the players and the rest of the city for generations.

What if Bank of America and Wachovia hadn't done so many ill-advised deals? What if Wachovia had received a government bailout? What if regulators and ratings agencies had done more to rein in risks in the financial system?

The damage to the city—can't be understated. Hundreds of bankers— maybe a neighbor down the street, maybe a close friend, maybe even a spouse—lost their jobs. Shareholders, many of whom had held

Charlotte bank stocks for decades, watched tens of billions of dollars in market value and dividends seemingly evaporate over night.

Take Bank of America's once-lucrative dividend. In 2007, the bank paid out $10.9 billion to its shareholders. In 2013, the payout had shrunk to $1.7 billion.

"It was a stock that had been handed down generation to generation," says Jon Finger, a Bank of America shareholder who has been critical of the bank's management and board of directors. "A number of people faced real changes in their retirement."

And of course, there is the ongoing blow to Charlotte's image and can-do spirit. The city lost the headquarters of a Fortune 500 company with the sale of Wachovia, a blue-chip North Carolina institution that had earned a sparkling reputation across the country. Bank of America, which once conquered some of the country's biggest banks, became a national punching bag.

Among the many lessons learned in the crisis: Charlotte realized that its place in the banking world wasn't as lofty as it had once thought. Most of the decisions concerning the fate of the city's banks were made by lawyers in Midtown Manhattan and regulators inside the Beltway. The city got a taste of what San Francisco, Birmingham, Atlanta, and Boston experienced when Charlotte banks snapped up their hometown institutions.

Six years later, Charlotte has fewer banking jobs and less clout in the financial world, but it has shown an impressive resilience. An array of financial firms have set up shop in the city, giving many former employees from the big banks a place to land. Other industries such as the energy sector are also picking up some of the slack.

Memories of the nerve-wracking and wearying days of the financial crisis are fading, but a glance at some of the *Charlotte Observer*'s photos from 2008 and 2009 will bring back a rush of emotions to anyone who lived in Charlotte during those dizzying times.

In one shot, Wachovia executives Bob Steel and Ben Jenkins, both obviously emotionally drained, prepare for an employee meeting announcing the Wells Fargo merger, as Wells Fargo CEO John Stumpf looks on with empathy.

In another, after the close of the Wells Fargo deal, a rolling electronic stock ticker on a College Street tower flashes the listing for Wachovia: "N/A."

Not available.

RICK ROTHACKER is a business reporter at the *Charlotte Observer*. He received the Gerald Loeb Award for beat writing in June 2009 for his coverage of Wachovia and has also won awards from the Society of American Business Editors and Writers and the North Carolina Press Association. He is the author of *Banktown: The Rise and Struggles of Charlotte's Big Banks*. Rothacker lives in Charlotte with his wife, Jen, and their two sons.

Friends & Family

A Sense of Place

MARK DE CASTRIQUE

"WE NEED A PLACE in Charlotte that looks like 1955 Mississippi." The BBC producer made the demand without doubt that the city could pass for one of the most impoverished regions of the country. Obviously, he hadn't been reading the chamber of commerce brochures.

His television documentary was telling the story of the key murders that sparked the American civil rights movement, and he needed a location to dramatize the killing of Emmett Till, the fourteen-year-old African American teenager savagely slaughtered in 1955 in Mississippi for allegedly flirting with a white woman. As the project's production manager, I was responsible for finding a setting that might pass for the rural Mississippi Delta somewhere within the radius of our shining beacon of the New South. I personally knew only one spot linking Charlotte to the landscape of its rural roots.

I parked my car in the overgrown driveway, long bare of gravel. I was glad to see the old farm standing, its fallow fields yet to be paved over or the house and barn razed to grow progress. All was still there. The small,

single-story home sat neglected and forgotten under the shade of two towering oaks. I looked at it through the eyes of the BBC producer. Filmed at
night, when Emmett Till had been snatched from his great-uncle's house,
the location could work.

As I stepped into the patchy grass of the front yard, the roar of a jet
drowned the sound of passing traffic on Little Rock Road, and for a split-
second, an ascending plane blocked the late afternoon sun, throwing its
shadow over the property. The shadow of death, I thought, a weapon just
as effective as a gun for killing off a way of life, for destroying this land that
had been in the same family since the king of England granted it to them in
the 1700s. Fewer than eight miles from downtown Charlotte, the Bigham
farm had survived a revolution, a civil war, a depression, but not prosperity.

The attack came from the air. As Charlotte boomed in the 1970s and
1980s, the farm land in the southwest corner of the county was sacrificed for
runways so that large domestic jets and then international carriers could
swoop in, bringing the treasures of commerce and fueling the growth that
some like these simple farmers saw as malignant. But, their voices were few
and faint.

My Aunt Carol, one of my father's four sisters, had married into the
Bigham family and lived in a house a quarter mile down the road. My two
brothers and I would come from our home in the western North Carolina
mountains to visit during the summers. A few weeks of farm chores were
exciting to us, and our two cousins enjoyed playing with their mountaineer
relatives.

The old farmhouse in front of me had become the residence of the
unmarried siblings from two generations back—my uncle's three aunts and
two uncles. The sisters, Ruth, Irma, and Mae, kept house, cooked the meals,
canned the vegetables; the two brothers worked the fields and tended the
livestock.

Every morning we cut up through the pasture from my uncle's to help
slop the hogs and feed the horses. Joe Bigham was in his late fifties then,
the baby of the household. He took charge of the hogs. His older brother

Charlie spent his time farming the fields with the horses. They were his children. He'd tried a tractor once and given it up. He'd sooner hitch up his team behind the plow than eat. Folks used to stop their cars along the road and watch him work, like watching history, like seeing a steam locomotive climb a grade long after the diesels had stolen the tracks.

I walked around the rear of the house and into the barn. Ghosts whispered from the empty stalls and I listened. They would tell their tales for a few weeks more and then everything—farmhouse, shed, barn— would be leveled. The brothers and sisters had been gathered into the cemetery of Steele Creek Presbyterian Church, reunited with the bones of their forebears going back more than two hundred years.

A company in Atlanta owned the farm now and planned to bury its heritage beneath a layer of asphalt, turning the once-fertile land into a holding pen for the automobiles of the air travelers—a parking lot where "long-term" meant a week or two, not centuries.

A college professor once studied the dialect of the Bigham family. He claimed it was more Old English than Southern, akin to the speech found on the Outer Banks or in mountain hollows where isolation kept accents and idioms separate from the changes of the common tongue. In the silence of the barn, I could hear Joe and Charlie talking of things they would do next *Chuesday* or of eating a *chuna* sandwich for supper. Charlie's favorite words must have been embedded in the plank walls somewhere. *Gee* and *haw.* They would turn his horses right and left with the precision of rack-and-pinion steering.

I crouched beside a rusted pulley that must have been part of a block-and-tackle rig Charlie used to hoist feed above the stalls. I brushed aside the decaying leaves of last autumn to reveal the whole assembly: a simple tool consisting of a chain looped around a nine-inch wheel. That was about the extent of Charlie's use for technology. The irony crossed my mind. Here I was scouting a location for a documentary, and Charlie had been the first person I ever saw on television whom I actually knew. National network television, no less.

I don't know how he met the circus people. Someone, maybe a friend from church who worked at the old coliseum on Independence Boulevard, passed Charlie's name along to them. The man and woman were foreign is all I remember. They had some Slavic last name jammed full of consonants. They needed a handler for their horses during the two weeks they were in Charlotte, and Charlie was recommended. The husband and wife team were acrobats on horseback and at times they performed on four horses abreast.

I doubted if Charlie had ever been to a circus, but he knew horses and that was a bond transcending cultural differences. For every performance, Charlie held the horses just outside the ring where the man or woman could spring atop them. Charlie bought new bib overalls for the occasion and seemed just as proud as the riders in their gold-sequined costumes.

Two weeks working with the circus should have been adventure enough, but it didn't stop there. Charlie invited his employers to the farm to see his plow horses, and something about the place captured their fancy. Maybe it was all Charlie—his sincerity, his love for horses regardless of pedigree. Anyway, the husband and wife asked if they could train there during the off-season. They toured with the smaller, regional circuses that booked cities outside those covered by Ringling Brothers, and they concentrated their performances during the winter while the Ringling Brothers troupe quartered in Florida.

Charlie's new friends set up a circus ring behind the barn, complete with the aerial rigs used for practicing flips and complicated dismounts. They were there when my brothers and I came for our annual summer holiday. Our two cousins, Billy and Betty Jane, could hardly wait to show us their dream come true. How many kids can boast of a real circus in their backyard?

The performers practiced early morning and evening to avoid the heat. We'd lie in the pasture, sucking on grass stems and watching the woman with long blond hair turn somersaults and backflips. The exciting moments came when she would shed the harness and balance on two galloping horses, arms outstretched as if wings, hair blowing in the wind. She looked like a goddess in the golden sunlight. We would break out in spontaneous applause when she executed a particularly spectacular trick and gasp in horror on those occasions when our goddess toppled from the steeds and sprawled in the dust.

Charlie always ran for the horses, and the husband would kneel beside his wife, first listening to a stream of foreign words we didn't understand but knew were bad, then calmly asking what went wrong and would she want to go back into the safety rig. Sometimes she did, other times she didn't; but she always, always got back up on the horses.

"Those circus people," as the sisters called them, lived in a caravan trailer behind the barn. At first they kept to themselves, but after a week, they began bringing iced tea and lemonade up to the house in the afternoons. That earned them an invitation to the dinner table, dinner being served at high noon every day but Sundays when church delayed the meal till one. Then extra towels were laid out in the bathroom for washing up, and the final measure of acceptance was the offer of a tub bath on *Chuesdays* and Fridays.

In the evenings, Ruth, Irma, and Mae would come out after the supper dishes had been washed to watch the practice. They'd sit in their cotton dresses on three lawn chairs placed arm to arm. Joe spread a blanket for us kids and then fetched a watermelon from the field across the fence. About the time dusk forced the circus people to quit for the day, the lightning bugs would rise up from the grass and create a twinkling universe under the blossoming stars. We'd catch them in jars until my uncle's whistle came from across the pasture, signaling our day was over.

Sometimes a late afternoon or evening thunderstorm would send us scurrying for the safety of the farmhouse. If the winds weren't blowing too hard, we'd sit out on the side porch behind the protection of the screen walls and listen to the old folks talk of the past. The three sisters squeezed together in the glider and set a slow back-and-forth rhythm that flowed with the languid conversation. Joe and Charlie sat in rocking chairs, Charlie always nearer the screen door, and the creak of their wooden rockers and the squeak of the glider's springs created a musical lullaby that mingled with the soft whispery voices.

It was on a Friday night, the last Friday before Mom and Dad were driving down the mountain to get us, that the news was sprung. The woman came from the bathroom with her hair wrapped in a towel and a red robe gathered around her muscular body. The sound of rockers and glider stopped in unison as if a conductor's baton had waved them into silence. True, she wore fewer clothes when she performed in the circus, but that was more like a fancy bathing suit. Here she stood in shocking proximity to two bachelor men and their purer-than-pure sisters.

The breeze of the advancing storm rose and threatened to lift the lower corner of the robe. I looked at the women in the glider. Their eyes grew as large as crab apples, and for once their cataracts didn't impede their vision.

The circus lady nonchalantly pressed the robe to her thigh and turned away from the wind. "Char-LEE," she said, emphasizing the second syllable. "I am so happy. Stephan has told me you are coming with us."

We all looked at Charlie. The woman could have been standing there nude or lying dead, and we would have still looked at Charlie. Irma chirped like an injured bird. Charlie's face went as red as the forgotten robe, as red as the center of a vine-ripened watermelon. He stared down at his hands like he had just discovered them. The bony knuckles whitened as he gripped the arms of the chair.

"Thinkin' bout it," he mumbled. "After the crop's in. Thinkin' bout it."

"You'll love the circus," said the woman, oblivious that the porch had become as somber as a funeral parlor. "It's like . . . it's like," she hesitated, groping for the right English word, "it's like your family."

Like our family? I thought. My own family? The idea seemed so crazy. What could we do in the circus?

"Thinkin' bout it," repeated Charlie, and started slowly rocking.

"I'd better get dressed and back to the trailer before the storm comes," the woman said.

The storm was coming all right. Joe was the first to break the painful silence. "I'll run you kids home in the truck. Get you in before the rain." He stood up and looked at me to follow.

I was ten, old enough to know I didn't want to be there when the words started pouring. I nodded to my brothers and we politely said goodbye. My cousin Billy, who must have been five, started to protest, but Joe reached down and pulled him to his feet so swiftly that the cry died in his throat.

Charlie held his ground.

For eight weeks that winter, he traveled with the circus. One night my Aunt Carol called long distance to say the weekly television show *Big Top* was featuring those circus people on the upcoming Saturday broadcast.

We didn't have a TV, but Mr. and Mrs. Hinkel, the retired people who lived higher up the mountainside, owned one of those Sylvanias with the soft-glow halo around the picture tube. My brothers and I had watched *Big Top* before at their house.

On the big day, our whole family walked up the mountain. In the Hinkels' living room, *Big Top* came on, with its calliope music rattling the thin Sylvania speakers.

We didn't have to wait in suspense. For the very first act, the ringmaster announced the greatest acrobats on horseback whose daring stunts had only been surpassed by their daring escape from behind the Iron Curtain.

Suddenly, the screen filled with a galloping horse and on its back stood the lady I'd seen behind the barn. Even in fuzzy black and white, she looked magnificent. My brothers and I cheered as she flipped backward and forward. Then her husband was on a horse beside her, and they jumped across, changing places, while the horses ran around the ring. We all edged closer to the set.

At the end, when the husband and wife had flawlessly performed their final stunts across the backs of four horses and dismounted in twisting, turning somersaults to the enthusiastic applause of the audience, the camera picked up the lanky form of an old man in bib overalls running out to grab the reins.

"Charlie!" I cried.

Another jet rumbled overhead, vibrating the rusted tin roof. I looked around, and sensed the emptiness. I'd cleaned out what had been waiting for me to rescue.

What remained was as far removed from me as the Mississippi Delta.

MARK DE CASTRIQUE is a video/film producer and the author of two mystery series: the Asheville-based Sam Blackman novels and the Buryin' Barry mysteries set in his fictional mountain town of Gainesboro. Other novels include the Washington DC thriller, *The 13th Target,* the Raleigh-based sci-fi thriller, *Double Cross of Time,* and two novels for young adults. Mark and his wife, Linda, have lived in Charlotte for over thirty years.

Fred Kirby:
Charlotte's Singing Cowboy

ANN WICKER

SAY "GIVE ME THE HIGH SIGN" to a Charlottean of a certain age and chances are he or she will put the back of a hand up under his or her chin and waggle their fingers at you.

No, this is not a gang sign — exactly. It is a symbol of the legacy of one of Charlotte's heroes. But let me start at the beginning.

In 1927 or so, a young man went with his uncle to a Columbia, South Carolina, store to get his guitar fixed. That store was across the street from radio station WIS, which had been on the air for about a year. The young man's uncle sent him over to see the station while he (the uncle) was doing some other business. Finding the front office deserted, the young man wandered into one of the studios with his newly repaired guitar and started to play and sing. He was startled when his uncle and another man came into the room and told him he "had the job." The young man with the guitar was Fred Kirby. The stranger who gave him the job was Charles Crutchfield. Crutchfield later moved to Charlotte to be an announcer on WBT, a powerful radio station heard up and down the East Coast, where he would eventually become general manager.

The son of a Methodist minister, Fred Kirby was born in Charlotte but spent his childhood in South Carolina. Some months after breaking into the business at the Columbia radio station, Kirby moved to Charlotte to play music on WBT, beginning his long association with the radio station and later its sister television station, WBTV.

But before he really settled down in the Queen City, Kirby left Charlotte for a while and moved on to other jobs in radio in Cincinnati, Chicago, and elsewhere. Along the way, he became known as "the Victory Cowboy" during World War II, as he helped sell millions of dollars worth of war bonds. In an interview I did with him in 1980, he told me that one of his proudest moments was riding in Harry Truman's inaugural parade in 1949. That parade was also the beginning of his association with a horse named Calico, a black and white stallion presented to Kirby for the occasion. After the first Calico went to the great rodeo in the sky, Kirby owned a number of other horses with the same name.

By the time WBTV signed on in July of 1949, Kirby had moved back to Charlotte and was again appearing on WBT, sometimes with the Briarhoppers, a popular string band Crutchfield had put together some years before.

In 1951, when the television station started producing local programming, Kirby became the host of the first children's television program in the state, *Junior Rancho*. With his trademark white hat and cowboy outfit, Kirby became popular for his positive approach and friendly smile, making it easy for parents to welcome him into their living rooms.

Just as WBT was one of the most powerful and most listened-to radio stations on the East Coast, WBTV became a powerhouse television station. From the beginning, WBTV was affiliated with the CBS network, although in those early years programming also included popular shows from NBC, ABC, and other networks.

It's hard to overestimate the influence of WBTV and the television personalities associated with the station in Charlotte and the region through the Fifties, Sixties, and Seventies. With the strongest broadcast signal, WBTV probably reached more households than its main competitor, WSOC-TV, which had signed on to the airwaves in 1957.

Kirby wasn't the only local entertainer to become a television celebrity thanks to WBTV. Among others, Loonis McGlohon, Arthur Smith, Betty Feezor, and Clyde "Cloudy" McLean also became regional (and Smith and McGlohon, national) stars, thanks in part to their exposure on WBTV. McGlohon and Smith were both heard first on WBT. McGlohon became an internationally known songwriter and pianist, and folks like Frank Sinatra and Margaret Whiting covered his songs. He partnered with composer Alec Wilder and brought *American Popular Song with Alec Wilder and Friends* to a national audience through a show on National Public Radio. Smith, in his many television ventures on WBTV and elsewhere, showcased regional and nationally known musicians and pioneered the musical variety show. Feezor's long-running, mid-day home-making show made her a popular figure among women who were trying to balance home and work lives. The tall, lanky McLean presided over a weather map upon which he had to hand-draw the predictions.

Perhaps to compete with Kirby and the powerful WBTV, or just to follow the national trend of the time, WSOC-TV hired Brooks Lindsay in 1959 to host a children's show called *Clown Carnival*. Lindsay created a hobo-ish clown character, Joey the Clown, who was perhaps a little more edgy than the straight-shooting, singing cowboy personified by Kirby. Although there was certainly a rivalry between the two stations, the two men shared a philosophy of kindness and generosity. Lindsay signed off each of his shows with Joey the Clown saying, "Be nice to each other and get along with each other, because all we have in this old world is each other."

In the early days, both shows had live audiences — children's birthday parties and groups of children from schools — with minimal sets. Kirby led them in singing songs, and Joey the Clown had them make "Joey Trees" out of rolled-up newspapers.

Over the years, Kirby's different shows often featured his beloved side-kick, the late Jim Patterson (known as Uncle Jim). However, according to *Stay Tuned Boys & Girls*, a documentary on North Carolina's most prominent children's show hosts, Joey the Clown broke new ground in local children's television programming with his usual sidekick, "Miss Ginger," a Miss North Carolina runner-up who wore tight mini-dresses.

Kirby's forte, of course, was his music—a *Charlotte Observer* story published after he died mentioned that he'd written more than five hundred songs—but he was also known for his work with charities and children. Here he led by example. He was always visiting children in hospitals, leading Christmas parades, visiting department stores, and making appearances for charity functions. In the parades, he usually rode Calico (or one of his "descendants"). A side gig for Kirby was his position as "marshal" at Tweetsie Railroad, a theme park located between Blowing Rock and Boone in the North Carolina mountains. There his fans could see him in person and have their picture taken with him, not to mention ride the restored train with him as he saved the day when train robbers "attacked" or other catastrophes occurred.

As a child, I idolized Fred Kirby. He played guitar and sang songs, he smiled constantly, and he was friendly to children but never talked down to them. After I grew up and became a newspaper reporter, I jumped at the chance to interview Kirby. It was Christmastime 1980, and he appeared at a Woolworth's. He outdrew Santa that day. Folks lined up to see him, to introduce their kids to him, to have a photo taken—sometimes three generations of fans at once. No matter the age, he always called his fans "his children."

At the time, we talked about his longstanding appeal—even then he was still doing a television show—and he laughed. "You can't fool a child," he said. "They can tell a phony."

When, much later, I wrote about Kirby after he died in 1996, I observed that at least two generations of folks around Charlotte were inspired to volunteer to help others by Kirby's standard of giving back to the community.

But back to the high sign. By the time he finally retired from television in the 1980s, Kirby had hosted a number of different shows with different themes and sets, the most popular of which was *The Little Rascals Club* in the 1970s. At the height of its popularity, this show drew some 200,000 viewers every week. The show, broadcast at noon on Sundays, featured *Our Gang* comedy shorts, which had been made mostly in the Thirties and early Forties. Friends have told me of bugging their parents to hurry home from church so they could see the show.

One of these shorts (some sources indicate it was 1935's *Anniversary Trouble*, which also featured an appearance by soon-to-be Oscar-winner Hattie McDaniel) introduced the "high sign," as demonstrated by several of the main characters, including Spanky and Stymie as they parodied fraternal organizations with their Wood Chuck Club. Uncle Jim and Kirby co-opted the finger wave as a repeated bit of stage business on the show.

The Little Rascals' high sign still connects Kirby's fans near and far as they share the memory of a generous man and a true hero.

Writer and editor **ANN WICKER** was in the newspaper and magazine business for many years. A graduate of Davidson College, she holds an MFA in creative writing from Queens University of Charlotte. She edited *Making Notes: Music of the Carolinas,* a nonfiction anthology idea she took to Novello Festival Press. She works with writers as an editor and writing coach. Her own work has appeared in a number of regional magazines. Her blog is www.eastoakmedia.com/ThatsAllSheWrote.

Welcome Home, Brother

SHARON RAYNOR

PERHAPS MY WORK with Vietnam veterans was predestined. The last American troops withdrew from Vietnam on March 29, 1973; I was born the very next day (which is now the official "Welcome Home Vietnam Veterans Day"). As the daughter of a Vietnam veteran, I was constantly asking questions about the war which were answered by my family with silence. I learned from my father that a child should always be willing to listen, even if nothing is being said. Silence can be profound; even silence has its own story to tell. My father's silence was explained by his diary and by photographs he brought home to Charlotte from the war. Hidden away from prying eyes, these documents only told part of my father's story.

When I got older, I went in search of the rest. I was intrigued by how this culture of Vietnam veterans somehow provided comfort for my father that he couldn't get from his family or from me, his own daughter. But he and his fellow veterans are forever united by the silence of war.

War reduces everything to silence. Every soldier's grave a place
too loud for sleep.
—E. Ethelbert Miller, "First Poem"

My interest in Vietnam stems from wanting to know the experiences of men who fought in Vietnam and lived to return to the same communities they had left, though they came back as very different men. They tell of being drafted or enlisting for service, of leaving homes and segregated communities for integrated battalions, of fighting for civil liberties, freedoms and racial justice abroad while the civil rights movement was proceeding at home. They tell of violent loss and disappointing homecomings, followed by decades of silence, of personal readjustments and survival. Because they were among the first to serve in fully integrated troop battalions in a combat zone, their stories have special significance.

As I continued on this journey with my father and so many other veterans, I found answers to my questions about war and silence. While I learned to listen to the silences of their stories, I also learned how to hear the story that my own silence tells.

> *What I want for my daughter, she shall never have:*
> *A world without war, a life untouched by the bigotry*
> *and hate, a mind free to carry a thought up to the light of pure possibility.*
> —W.D. Ehrhart, "Why I Don't Mind"

Our journey brought us to Charlotte Motor Speedway on Saturday, March 31, 2012. I spent my thirty-ninth birthday weekend with more than 62,000 Vietnam veterans and their families at the Welcome Home Vietnam Veterans Celebration. After months of planning, this event, said to be the largest gathering of Vietnam veterans ever assembled in North Carolina, had finally arrived. Nearly fifty years earlier, approximately 216,000 men and women left North Carolina to serve in Vietnam. About 1600 of them didn't make it home. The ones who did make it back never received a proper homecoming. The time had finally come to thank them for their service and sacrifice, and the city of Charlotte planned to do so in the grandest way imaginable.

As I was driving from Durham to Charlotte on the Thursday before the big day, I heard a radio broadcaster say that the final preparations for the Welcome Home Vietnam Veterans Celebration at Charlotte Motor Speedway were underway. The broadcaster asked motorists traveling through Charlotte on I-85 North to move aside if they saw the motorcycle and police motorcade escorting a replica of the Vietnam Memorial Wall (the Traveling Wall) from Belmont to the speedway. I couldn't help but feel a bit emotional—the big day for Vietnam veterans, like my father, was almost here at last.

> *If there must be trouble, let it be in my day, so that my child may have peace.*
> —Thomas Paine

Charlotte's "superspeedway" can be seen from any direction. This monumental, almost monstrous complex, is located an ironic thirteen miles outside of the city at the old Charlotte Fairgrounds. Home of NASCAR with a seating capacity of 135,000, the speedway was deemed the perfect location for the grand Welcome Home Vietnam Veterans Celebration. Besides, over the years, it has been the chosen site for music videos and television commercials, world movies, auto shows, and swap meets. With its grandstands, luxury seats, condominiums, nighttime racing, ten-acre Fan Zone, and reputation as "the greatest place to see the race," the veterans would be welcomed home in style.

My father and family started our journey on Saturday at 6 a.m., determined to make our way to the speedway in advance of the anticipated rush. Unfortunately, on what was to be a day that so many Vietnam veterans had been waiting for, there was torrential rain. But nothing would stop this event. After a quick bite to eat, we grabbed our umbrellas, ponchos, and bottles of water, and headed out. It was 7:30 when we parked at the speedway. The gates were opening at 9 a.m. for festivities that started at 11 a.m. Since my father uses a motorized chair for mobility, we found a parking space close to the enormous structure that would soon reach out and embrace North Carolina's warriors.

We entered the gates in the pouring rain, and met and talked to several other veterans who also had arrived early. We noticed an old Chevy van that was parked close by. A double-amputee vet moved much quicker than we, as we helped my father dismount his chair. We all walked toward the entrance gates in the pouring rain. I asked the stranger, "Are you here with your family?" He looked toward me and responded, "No, I'm alone." I held my umbrella over him as we moved at a snail's pace through the gate. I eventually said, "You can spend the day with me and my family." He looked at me rather oddly and expressed his appreciation. We finally made it through the gates and into the speedway. The stranger rolled away in the opposite direction, and I softly said, "Welcome home, sir. Thank you for your service." A deep admiration grew within me as I realized what he sacrificed during the war and how far he traveled alone just to be a part of this celebration, perhaps his first homecoming. The rain continued, and my father reminded me that today's weather was nothing compared to being in Vietnam during monsoon season, when it could rain for weeks if not months at a time.

As we entered, we saw the world's largest HDTV, spanning 200 feet wide and 80 feet tall, showing the young faces of men who served. It was astonishing to see the images of so many young faces of those who had served our country so very long ago projected on that larger-than-life screen.

The motorcycle club Rolling Thunder opened the ceremony with a grand entrance. Local motorcycle clubs were a conspicuous presence that day, as they are such a huge part of the Vietnam veteran culture. Because many motorcyclists were expected, the rules of the celebration had been communicated to them. They were told not to ride on the actual track but to stay on the apron just below the track and to avoid speeds exceeding 35 mph.

These rules caused some intense feelings that day. Some motorcyclist were determined not to follow the safety rules and continued to edge their way onto the track. Besides, they had ridden for miles and miles, from all across the state of North Carolina to be a part of this once-in-a-lifetime celebration of their service and sacrifice. Perhaps some were drawn to this event, even more because it was held at the speedway, one of Charlotte's main attractions and the home of NASCAR.

Amidst all the ceremony and display, there was a tremendous out-pouring of community spirit. The Veterans Administration services were present to assist veterans and their families, a wreath was laid at the Wall to remember all those who had perished in the war, a military flyby astonished the crowd, and paratroopers made an appearance to thundering applause. The musical performances by the 82nd Airborne Choir, George Clinton, and the Parliament Funkadelics had the crowd singing and dancing.

The sentiment of the day, "Welcome home, brother. I'm glad you made it back," was shared with friends, acquaintances, and strangers, passed between double amputees and disabled veterans, like my father. Regardless of whether they made the trip alone, with families, or by the busload, veterans exchanged handshakes, hugs, laughs, and tears; they were welcomed home by strangers and by cards from children across the nation. Families everywhere watched as their veterans were reunited with long-lost friends and comrades.

For many years, my father longed to find a veteran he served with or who at least served in some of the same locations. Luckily for him, a man named Jimmy drove by on a scooter with a sign that read, "Bearcat 1968, 5th BN 41st Artillery Brigade." The two of them sat and talked, sharing memories of Bearcat and looking at old photos of young soldiers. It was a highlight of the day. Two men, one black and the other white, who met decades ago in a foreign land, defended our country, and pro-tected each other from the perils of war, survived and today welcomed each other home. The event was a wonderful tribute to those who sacrificed so much for our freedoms.

He who is a friend, is a friend always, and brothers are born for adversity.
— Proverbs 17:7

Sadly, late in the day, and despite the many warnings to the motorcyclists, there was a tragic accident. As festivities ended and people were leaving, motorcyclists were asked to proceed slowly out of the speedway. But some stayed for that last chance to finally ride the speedway track. Three motorcyclists were doing laps around the track, headed in opposite directions. They crashed into each other and were immediately rushed to the hospital.

Two of them were veterans celebrating their homecoming, which within seconds turned into their tragic homegoing. They survived Vietnam, only to die perhaps doing what they most loved: riding. It added a note of sadness to a day that was already too full of reminders of how precious and short life can be. As the news about the deadly crash spread through the exiting crowd, it dampened uplifted spirits on the rainiest day Charlotte had seen in quite some time.

We returned to my house and all fell into a deep cathartic sleep.

The celebration continued the next morning at a local restaurant in Charlotte where we had Sunday breakfast, as veterans found each other for more conversation. There were stories about growing up on a farm in Oxford, North Carolina, before leaving for the war. Two men who had served in the same unit in Vietnam were reunited after forty years. They travelled to Charlotte together for that homecoming they long desired. We laughed with them, took photos, and my sisters and I secretly paid for their breakfast. Just that gesture alone, by strangers they just met, brought tears to their eyes. The bear hugs were tremendous and heartfelt, as we whispered, "Welcome home. Thank you for your service."

As we made our way out of the restaurant after many rounds of hugs and handshakes, we ran into more veterans outside. My father beamed with joy, as he finally felt at home and appreciated. The weekend was more than just a long-overdue homecoming for Vietnam veterans. It was a time of remembrance and healing for everyone whose lives have been touched and affected by war. The city of Charlotte found the words to finally say, "Welcome Home," to our state's Vietnam veterans.

> *Words have weight — you bear with me the weight of my words,*
> *suffering whatever pain this burden causes you — in silence. I bow to you.*
> —bell hooks, *remembered rapture*

SHARON RAYNOR is associate professor of English at Johnson C. Smith University and an adjunct instructor at the Center for Documentary Studies and Continuing Education at Duke University. She has written and directed two oral history projects about combat veterans in rural North Carolina, "Breaking the Silence" and "Soldier-to-Soldier." Her community scholarship and publications focus on the discourse of trauma, silence, and identity in Vietnam War studies.

Headed Home

Adapted from Losing My Sister

JUDY GOLDMAN

JANUARY 6, 2006. The day of the funeral. I haven't slept in too many nights to count. I've got a cold. My voice is just about gone. I feel hazy. Tired. Need propping up. I have to take the day slowly.

Daughter Laurie, son-in-law Bob, granddaughters Lucy and Zoe are staying with us. Laurie leaves early to observe at a preschool for the twins for next fall. They're moving from Durham to Charlotte this summer. Bob is trying hard to take care of the girls and relieve me of any responsibility. He's being quietly helpful. I open the refrigerator to take out orange juice and he sweeps in behind me, scoops up the carton, and fills their sippy cups. I ask Henry if it's too early for me to start getting dressed for the funeral. He says it's not too early. I'm the one who's always on time, and my husband's the one who's always late. He thinks that if we're invited to someone's house at eight, it means he should start getting ready at eight. But today, I make him the expert on time.

I put on a purple-ish turtleneck sweater and black pantsuit. It's what I'd planned to wear. But when I look in the mirror, I see that between the last time I wore the suit and this morning it has gone out of style. The shoulder pads are way too big and the jacket way too long. Hoping I'm wrong and my outfit is really just fine, I walk back into the kitchen and ask Henry what he thinks. He shakes his head, says it doesn't look so great. Now what? I have no idea what to wear to my sister's funeral. If it were my funeral, she'd have just the right outfit.

I pull out my lavender suede jacket, my lavender silk sweater, and my taupe pants. (Later, when I look around the synagogue during the service, it will be obvious I'm the only woman in the entire place not wearing black and one of the few wearing pants.)

Everyone is ready. Suits, ties, good shoes. Heavy coats. We leave the twins with two neighborhood friends. Both girls are crying hysterically. I'm worried about them, but don't want to let my dismay take over. I could easily let anything take over.

Son Mike and daughter-in-law Brooke, who've left their daughter Tess with Brooke's mother, pick up Laurie and Bob, and the four of them follow Henry and me down Providence Road to Temple Israel.

We gather in the chapel: my family, my brother Donald and his daughter, my sister's family (her husband Chuck, their four sons, their wives and children), assorted cousins. The rabbi pins a black ribbon on each of our jackets. Then he instructs us to tear them — a sign, he says, that someone has been torn from our midst. How in the world am I going to get through this? I never should have agreed to speak today. I keep reminding myself that I can back out at any point.

We're led into the sanctuary. It's filled with people. Even up in the balcony. Brenda would be touched. My main preoccupation, though, is keeping my emotions at bay. I concentrate on the stained glass windows. The temple is new, so the windows are new. I hate them. Why can't synagogues have *old* stained glass windows? Churchly ones. Why do we have to have modern everything? Why can't we have mahogany pews? I want colonial or Georgian. Not contemporary. It's working. I don't look at the casket in front of me, slightly to the right. I just keep hating those stained glass windows.

Suddenly, I realize the service has begun. The rabbi is chanting in Hebrew. Then he makes a few opening remarks, explaining the order of the service, including an introduction of the speakers: Brenda's husband, her sons, her sister.

He nods at me.

I rise from my seat, walk slowly and carefully up the steps to the altar, take my place behind the huge wooden podium, unfold my pages.

I cannot say a word. Tears are forming. If I open my mouth, I'll start crying.

I look up. It's quiet. And bright. All that sunlight pouring through the windows. Now I see that this stained glass has its own beauty and righteousness.

And then, in the wake of all that has gone on since Brenda's cancer recurred, I start speaking:

> Brenda, I think I must have begun to adore you the minute Mother and Daddy brought me home from the hospital, and I saw you for the first time. Then, we were beginning a life together. Now we're looking at ending a life together. Tender memories are swimming up, as if in shallow water.
>
> You're the one who sat for hours at the card table in the den on Eden Terrace, placing tiny seashells in intricate flower patterns, turning them into earrings and pins. That was me, sitting next to you, copying your every move, marveling at your artistic talent and business sense— qualities nameless to us then but irrevocably yours.
>
> You're the one who built a fishpond in our backyard. You were so young—yet you mixed and poured the wet concrete yourself. Our

parents might have wondered about that big, gluey hole in the middle of the yard, but now we know you were just demonstrating an early aptitude for landscaping.

You're the one who cooked with Mattie in the kitchen. Your peanut butter fudge. Your candy apples, which were so hard we had to crack them over the backs of wooden chairs to get them started.

You and I were always together. When our brother was supposed to babysit us but forgot and asked his girlfriend out on a date, Daddy insisted he take us along. There we were, at the drive-in, Donald and Mary Moore Sanders in the back seat, you and I in the front. All evening, we were adjusting the rearview mirror—and believe me, we saw a better movie in that mirror than anyone saw on the screen.

You were so much like our father—smart, wonderfully strong and steadfast and certain, *head*strong, brave (fearless, really), artistic, able to set a goal and achieve it. And you looked like him—that naturally curly hair, those green eyes, long legs. Like him, you were very sick before Thanksgiving, but you mustered every bit of strength you had to put on a magnificent Thanksgiving because you—like Daddy—knew it would be the last time your family would all be together in that house. Like his illness, your illness took a dramatic turn for the worse New Year's Eve. And like him, you breathed your last breath four days later.

But, even though everyone thought you were so like him, you were also like Mother—that extraordinary sense of style, not only in your clothes, but in the homes you created. Your sculpted flower arrangements, the gardens you designed and tended. Like Mother, you were pretty, graceful. Sweet.

Brenda, you're the one I shared a room with until the day you left for college. You and I were talking about that room as recently as eleven days ago—trying to recall every drawer. Of course, you had your dresser and I had mine. The one drawer we shared held our neckerchiefs and angora collars, the only clothes we could both wear and, of course, those were the ones we fought over. But we loved our room—the bachelor-

120

button wallpaper, the working fireplace, the tall brass lamp that separated our beds.

A few weeks ago, I had been walking with neighborhood friends and we'd parted halfway. I was heading back home alone. The days were growing shorter so it was already turning dark. I looked up at the sky. The moon hung just over the houses and there was a hazy ring around it, which meant we'd probably have rain the next day. All of a sudden, without any forethought or self-consciousness, I heard myself say out loud, as though I had this amazing and joyful news which I'd almost forgotten to tell: "Mother and Daddy, Brenda's coming!"

Next: David, Brian, Scott, and Danny walk up to the podium, and Scott steps to the microphone to read. I'm proud of Brenda's sons. She would be, too. In their dark suits and ties, they appear poised, confident. Early in his talk, Scott tells an old family story about his mom punishing him and Danny, probably for fighting. While the two brothers were banished to their shared bedroom, one asked the other, "Do you like Mom?" The other answered, "Naah."

At the end of his talk, Scott—with an affectionate nod toward his mom, whose presence I feel—refers back to that story: "And now I ask my brothers, do you like Mom?"

Then Chuck speaks. He wants to tell us a love story, he says. His speech is emotional and packed and detailed. His pain seems prismatic, like the rays of the sun shooting through those windows. How appropriate for it to be refracted through cracked glass.

The rest of the service I cannot remember. The rabbi speaks, the cantor chants, we read in unison, we stand, we sit. I look at the casket and try as hard as I can to picture Brenda lying inside.

Then it's over, and the family is ushered out of the temple as the rabbi follows behind, reading the 23rd Psalm. The psalm is a wave we ride, surfing those words up the aisle. The psalm carries us out of the sanctuary, through the vestibule, all the way out to the parking lot and our cars. It's a bitter-cold day. Unusual for Charlotte, even in January. This is the first I realize that I left my coat on the kitchen table.

Henry, Donald, and I drive together to the cemetery. We talk about Brenda. We're lost in remembering.

When I get out of the car at the cemetery, Laurie says, "Here, Mom," and helps me into her black coat. She slips into Bob's. We take our places under the canopy. I bend my body against the wind, hunch my shoulders so that the collar comes up around my face, and I stare at the hole. The rabbi drops a tablespoon of soil from Jerusalem into each of our palms and we take turns stepping forward and sprinkling it over the casket.

The rabbi prays and chants. Every word echoes.

Then he offers each of us the shovel and says that the first scoops of earth should be delivered with the back of the shovel because we're not building anything. Chuck and his sons go first. When Donald takes the shovel, I almost laugh because he's never held a shovel in his life and, by mistake, he spills dirt all over the bands crisscrossing the hole. Now he's trying to correct his mistake by cleaning the dirt off the bands, but it's not working.

Henry whispers to me, Do you want to take a turn shoveling dirt? I shake my head no. He asks if I want him to do it for me. I shake my head no again. I don't want to shovel dirt on Brenda's casket. I'm not ready for that part. There are other family members stepping forward.

The sound of the dirt dropping on the casket, over and over—it could be falling from a great distance.

After the service, friends stop me to talk. My hands are balled up in my coat pockets. Nearby, I hear Laurie and Mike planning a bowling outing with their cousins tonight. That feels right. I head for the car. Henry has left the doors unlocked—he and Donald are still visiting with people— and I slide in the front. I'm alone in the car, watching the gravesite.

The cemetery workers are shoveling in the rest of the dirt, filling the hole. They work fast. Their shoveling is definitely not symbolic. They mean business.

This place is cold and lonely and far from Brenda's neighborhood and mine. Once again, I hear myself speak out loud when there's no logical reason to be speaking out loud. As though a voice were coming from the dash or roof or floorboards of the car. But it's my voice and it's saying, "I'm so sorry I'm leaving you out here, Brenda."

One Saturday, late winter, the sky was white-gold. *That* bright. Brenda and I were in our early forties. Our parents had been dead a little over a year; it would be twenty years before Brenda's diagnosis of bile duct cancer. She had called the night before, excited about a place she'd heard about: Bell's Antiques in Cleveland County, near Shelby, North Carolina, about forty-five miles from Charlotte.

"We've got to go, Judy!" she'd said. "It's supposed to be great!"

Midmorning, we headed out, each of us dreaming of bargains. I hoped to find a wicker rocker for my screened porch. Brenda collected majolica, so she was in the market for a vase or pitcher. Also, she wouldn't mind finding an old wooden wheelbarrow decayed to gray, to plant ferns and Lenten roses in.

She was driving. I flicked on the heater, and warmth rushed to fill the car. We'd thrown our coats in the back seat. We were spinning stories, about our kids, her work, my work, all the things we'd saved up to tell.

We wondered if we'd been so busy talking we had missed the turn-off. Which led to kidding about how neither of us had a decent sense of direction, something we'd kidded about a million times before.

"If Chuck were with us," she said, "we'd be there."

"Oh my gosh," I said, "Henry would know exactly how to find it. He even knows east and west."

How we loved having the exact same conversation over and over, the comforting rhythms, how it could be almost a physical expression of affection, like adjusting the other's earring and touching her skin, too.

Down one country road, up another. We got caught behind a slow-moving tractor because the road was hilly and we couldn't pass. Surely, the antique store was up ahead. Finally, we spotted a gas station still in business. A man in overalls was pumping gas. Brenda pulled up beside him, rolled down her window, asked if he knew where Bell's Antiques was. He did. Yes, in*deed*. He went into great detail, pointing off into the distance, curving his body to show what the road would do, counting off with his fingers how many somethings we would pass.

Brenda thanked him, rolled her window up, pulled back onto the road. She smiled that smile that looked so much like our father. "I didn't understand a word he said!"

"Me neither!"

More laughs. All we could do was head back to the main road, then take a side road we should've seen before but didn't.

When signs for Shelby appeared, we thought maybe we would just follow them into town and ask there, but then we didn't see any more signs for Shelby.

Around noon, I said, "I'm getting hungry."

"Me, too," she said. Minutes later: "There!" She pointed to a crumbling sign on the side of the road. *B-B-Q* is all it said. "Want to try it?"

"Sure." We both loved finding out-of-the-way places to eat.

We turned off, followed a second *B-B-Q* sign onto a dirt road, bumped along till we came to a rundown restaurant, its wood siding peeling, roof missing shingles, sign knocked lopsided.

In the parking lot, we reached for our coats. I was thinking, This might be a little too out-of-the-way. I knew Brenda was thinking the same thing.

But the place was packed. A waitress, young and ponytailed, pointed us to a table by a window that was newly washed and sparkling. She handed us paper menus and named the specials, said we'd picked a nice day to eat lunch out and were we sisters, gosh, we sounded so much alike. Yes, we answered, we *are* sisters, and did she know where Bell's Antiques was? She didn't. We took our time reading the menu, ordering, eating, letting ourselves fall under the spell of pork and Brunswick stew cooked just right.

Back in the car, we felt renewed and determined. We didn't even take off our coats; we were so sure we were close. We drove, talked, laughed, well into the afternoon. The light came and went. And came again.

It turned out, we never did find Bell's. We'd been on the road five hours when we finally gave up and headed home. We'd been as lost as anyone could be. Yet we'd felt we could find our way anywhere. That's how full of love we were.

JUDY GOLDMAN's memoir, *Losing My Sister,* was a finalist for both the Southern Independent Booksellers Alliance's and *ForeWord Review*'s "Memoir of the Year." She's also the author of two novels and two poetry books. Her work has appeared in the *Washington Post, Real Simple, Southern Review, Kenyon Review, Ohio Review, Gettysburg Review, Prairie Schooner,* and *Shenandoah.* A Rock Hill native, she's lived in Charlotte since 1967.

In the Neighborhood

Veterans Park

RYE BARCOTT

TEE-TAWH, TEE-TAWH. The swing squeaks, back and forth, over and again. It's a peaceful sound, one that I love.

Sometimes it seems as though my daughter could play forever at Veterans Park. Her brown hair sails with the swing. Her name is Charlotte. Charlotte from Charlotte. She's three and has never had a haircut.

Before I became a parent, I heard that kids would change my perspective on time in dramatic ways. It's true, and it's hard for me to grasp that seven years earlier I was patrolling dusty streets in distant places, waiting to get shot at. The greatest tragedies I witnessed involved children. Some were as young as my daughter.

Now I am a veteran, and my daughter and I often go to Veterans Park on Saturday mornings. It's my favorite park. Charlotte delights in the big spray ground, the jungle gyms, and the swing. I enjoy the park's open spaces, and its gritty, welcome-all character.

Veterans Park is within jogging distance from our home, not far from Uptown, the city center. You wouldn't know you were in the city if you just happened to appear in the middle of the park, perched on the hill overlooking its playing fields. The city skyline is not visible. There are no shops, only houses and trees, a thick blanket of trees rolling toward South Carolina.

However, there are clues that we are in the South. The dirt on the baseball diamonds is a faint red clay. There is a church, City Church, on a nearby corner. Southern pines tower above the basketball courts. A willow oak shades the swing set and a squat brick building resembling a bunker. Years ago, my wife and I voted for the first time as Charlotte residents in that building.

A chain-link fence with three strands of barbed wire lines the northern perimeter of the park next to the community building. The fence separates the park from the origin of its namesake: a U.S. Army Reserve barracks. Two rows of Humvees are staged in formation, ready for the next call.

In Veterans Park my daughter has learned new things and made new friends from all over the world, a world she doesn't yet know. The first time she went down a slide was at this park, when a five-year-old girl coached her down, holding her hand. The girl was at the park by herself and was from "a not nice" part of Atlanta. She told us that weeks earlier she had moved to Charlotte to live with her grandmother.

Tee-tawh, tee-tawh, the swing goes with my little cupcake in it, smiling and laughing.

Another time, a small boy from a posh part of town taught Charlotte to swing in the "big-girls' swing" in Veterans Park.

Sometimes we run around the spray ground with kids from Eritrea. We've learned that many of the kids' families had fled war in the Horn of Africa and settled in a community on Central Avenue not far from the park. We meet someone new most times we visit—bankers, doctors, truck drivers, custodians. A homeless man occasionally sleeps on a bench. Often we hear unfamiliar languages.

Veterans Park is the New South. Here, you find people from all kinds of backgrounds, classes, and worldviews. The place does not forget history or pretend that everything is relative. It stands as a salute to those who have served. It celebrates our past and our history without making us a captive of it. It is a commons, welcome to all, where people meet to refresh old ties and build new ones. It doesn't matter who your daddy is, which car you drive, or what zip code you live in. You are welcome.

The New South is a place where things are possible. People are respected for who they are and what they aspire to be. You can come as you are, make friends, grow a family. You can rebuild.

Tee-tawh, tee-tawh. My daughter swings in the sun.

There was a time, not long ago, when I couldn't have appreciated any of this. Now, I don't want it to end. The thought of Charlotte growing older makes me a little sad, until I realize that we can come back to Veterans Park and discover new things. We can grow with this place, its towering trees, and the community around it.

RYE BARCOTT is the author of *It Happened on the Way to War,* which was named one of four best nonfiction books of 2011 by *Reader's Digest* and has been adopted in high school and college reading programs across the nation.

New Southern Blues

For Jonathan Ferrell (died 9/14/13, Charlotte, NC)

JANAKA B. LEWIS

"I cannot shoot the breeze today,"
 Said little Virgil B. McKay
"Cause in the streets of Charlotte town
 Another man has been gunned down."

Not armed was he, but charged toward who
He thought would help, the men in blue.
Unfortunately 'twas ill-received
Shots rang, then rang, then dead indeed.

"I cannot go to church today,"
 Said Mrs. Peggy Ann McCrae.
"What God is this," she moaned and sighed,
"Could let this life be cast aside?"

New South is where she made her home
Where sons of brown could safely roam.
3 boys had she, their father served
Until, life lost, his movement curbed

And so she carried them to stay
She heard, a safer place to play.

'Twas not to be, was Southern still,
Though not a field for them to till.
Instead, a street they couldn't roam
For fear The Lord would call them home
Another life she couldn't lose
Another verse of mama's blues.

Blue was the sky, red was the road
A city wanting to implode
But yet, expand and grow and rise
Until its buildings reached the skies.

New South, old pain
Old wounds explain
Woman afraid
A child's thoughts laid
Wide open so the world can see
A people not yet truly free

Progress, regress, and rest in peace
Southern lives lost, skylines increase.

JANAKA B. LEWIS, PhD, is an assistant professor of English who specializes in African American literature at the University of North Carolina at Charlotte. She is the author of a children's book, *Brown All Over*, and researches literary and cultural issues surrounding African American mobility and freedom. Born in Georgia, she attended Duke University, then moved to Chicago (the Midwestern South), before moving to the Charlotte area. She believes that all of these locations deem her a New Southerner.

College Downs

AIMEE PARKISON

BEFORE I MOVED to College Downs, people warned me it was one of the most eccentric neighborhoods in Charlotte. Wandering drunks, nuns, monks, and naked joggers keep traveling hidden pathways through the neighborhood, circling below the flight of the owl. I always think of it as *my owl*, even though it belongs to no one. I hear the owl every night, and in the fall, I see it almost every evening before it begins hunting at sundown.

Last night, the owl flew over the evergreens and perched on the lamp-post in the back of the neighbor's yard as my husband lit a fire. I'm hoping to see the owl again tonight, even though seeing the owl fills me with strange ideas about this place.

It's October, and my floodlight dahlias are still blooming! Pink and peach roses are still going strong. All over the neighborhood are gardens of flowers, vegetables, and berries. Pecan trees, peach trees, and wild pears grow along the woodland trails. The wild pears are small with a more intense flavor than those that are sold in the grocery store. The size of new potatoes, they clean up the teeth and stomach but cannot be swallowed. When eating wild pears, one must chew and chew and then spit. The meat is too fibrous to be digested, although the juice is delicious.

Sometimes I wonder if the drunks who hide in the woods at night know about the pears, or if they go to the dark to escape. Do the drunks have homes? At night, holding a little flashlight, I often walk the narrow trail in the dark, weaving through the tall trees and listening for voices. My eyes don't adjust well to darkness. It's hard for me, as I worry about falling. I worry about tripping over a root, or a foot.

"Oh, that guy," one of my neighbors, a professor of composition, says when I ask her about the man in the woods. "That drunk guy who sleeps in the trees? He's harmless. Everybody knows about him."

"What about his friend?"

"His friend?"

"He talks to me sometimes."

"What are you doing in the woods after dark?"

The trail is rocky and full of thick roots. It leads to a shopping center with a decent grocery store, a local coffee shop, a video-game shop with an arcade, a smoke shop with lots of pipes and hookahs on display, a drugstore, a doughnut shop, restaurants, and a large sports bar. In the midst of it all, behind the shopping center, the woods and its trails are full of wild-life — owls, deer, foxes, semi-tame hawks, jackrabbits, and a wild wolflike dog I once saw watching from the hill. All this wildlife wanders into the neighborhood, invading the lawns with the greatest gardens. Deer eat our tomato plants, and jackrabbits eat our lettuce. In late summer, when wild mint flowers, my yard transforms into a butterfly garden, alive with bright large wings of swallowtails, the hum of wasps and bees and darting hummingbirds.

My backyard fills with jackrabbits — adult rabbits and babies and rabbits in between adult and baby. I wonder if the owl hunts the rabbits or even the tiny silver fox I saw at twilight. On some nights, a one-armed raccoon walks up to my den's sliding-glass doors to look into my house as cats yowl. There are other cries in the night — animalistic howls. Night screams are normal sounds for anyone living in College Downs, as the party season turns drunken students into animals after dark. Intoxicated renters drive pickups and motorcycles and four-wheelers through the woods, forcing vehicles between trees along dark trails to avoid getting caught by the cops when going for a beer run or leaving the sports bar.

"Turn off that damn music!" an elderly neighbor yells from her house behind the trees.

All night, loud music has been blaring from speakers in the rented house next to hers.

I laugh, wondering what it means that I'm so happy about the woman yelling. She sounds really angry, and I'm glad she's willing to express her anger. But someone turns up the music even louder shortly after she complains.

As hours pass, I hear distant trains moving along the tracks, and just before daybreak the faraway sound of roosters crowing. I hear my owl, but I also hear other sounds, sounds just as intriguing, sounds that warn of trouble from the tribe of student renters. There are a lot of problems here lately, strange problems related to students. More students are living here than ever before. Approximately half of all the houses are now rentals, and in each rental, numerous students reside, some as actual renters and some as guests at the never-ending party circuit that fills our streets and lawns with strange caravans at night.

Numerous people are hiding in the trees at all hours, trespassers invading private lawns as they move from one party house to another. At 2 a.m., I hear voices talking outside my bedroom window, so I go outside to see what is happening. A group of students is congregating in my yard, using it as a pass through and stopping to smoke a joint. When they see me, they simply say, "We're here!" Of course, I have no idea who they are, but they seem to think "We're here!" is the only explanation needed.

More trespassers gather. As I wait inside my house, I'm watching from my windows. Soon, I see searchlights cutting through the woods. I hear police officers yelling through bullhorns as the searchlights cut through the darkness, the beams of light bouncing through the trees to reveal hundreds of people hiding in the shadows of branches. People begin screaming, running through the dark, as the police pursue them on foot. Several minutes later, there is silence and then the sounds of dozens of cars starting at once. Finally, the police leave and a caravan of fifty or more cars speed out of the neighborhood.

In the days that follow, I see evidence of bizarre churches invading the neighborhood, cults recruiting student followers and taking over rental houses closest to campus. Cults turn rental houses into makeshift churches where members come and go, some staying as if they are tenants. There are also rumors of some houses being converted into secret motels, where rooms can be rented by separate parties on a nightly, weekly, or monthly basis. I confess to first-hand knowledge of this. When I moved into my own house, I discovered closets littered with bright yellow no-trespassing signs and police warnings near an eviction notice and a flyer with the number of a local locksmith.

In the midst of all this chaos are tasteful, historical homes, picturesque, once inhabited by the founders of the university, and constructed by a renowned local builder, John Crosland Company. The company now develops commercial and industrial properties. However, in the early 1960s, when College Downs was just getting started, Crosland built high-quality brick ranch houses and split-levels elegantly positioned on large wooded lots.

Some of the faculty who live in the neighborhood are still teaching at the university. Other residents are retired or emeritus, friends and family of faculty, or people who have worked in administrative roles for decades. Many of these residents are members of a neighborhood association affectionately referred to as FOMB, "Friends of Miss Bonnie," a group dedicated to community improvement through university relations. FOMB is named after Bonnie Ethel Cone (June 22, 1907 – March 8, 2003), an American educator best known as the founder of the University of North Carolina at Charlotte. Bonnie Cone once lived in College Downs, even though her house was not on Bonnie Lane. Her former house, cradled by the very trees that overshadow its densely wooded lot, is one of the older houses on Sandburg Avenue, where I now live. Sandburg Avenue, unlike

137

Lewis Carroll Circle, is rapidly becoming a center for overflow university traffic. Students like to park in front of the Bonnie Cone house because it is a short walk to campus.

Because College Downs borders the southeast side of the University of North Carolina at Charlotte campus off of University City Boulevard, the neighborhood voted to restrict parking on Sandburg Avenue, Ogden Place, Nash Avenue, Nottoway Drive, Bonnie Lane, Joyce Kilmer Drive, and Robert Burns Court. Residents didn't really have a choice, because our neighborhood was becoming a parking lot with vehicles parked on both sides of the street, leaving only a narrow one-lane passage for vehicles and pedestrians. Of course, we have no sidewalks, like most Charlotte neighborhoods. The university has nearly 30,000 students, and the enrollment has been increasing by roughly a thousand students per year, as parking fees and rates for on-campus parking keep rising. Walking can be dangerous, as students overload houses, living six to ten in a four-bedroom residence, catering to dozens, if not hundreds, of "guests" on party nights, and these hungover guests must eventually follow the "walk of shame" back to campus dorms or their nearby apartments.

College Downs has always had a love-hate relationship with the university. The neighborhood, like all of the university-area housing developments and businesses, depends upon the university in a sort of symbiotic relationship. I first moved into College Downs in the summer of 2011, when I became captivated by its location, its charm, and its beauty. From my house, I am able to walk to everything I need — campus, bars, restaurants, grocery stores, and the local coffee shop. Almost every day, I witness drunken debauchery, amazingly diverse wildlife, rental houses hiding homegrown cults, and the occasional monk or nun walking through the neighborhood. For the most part, I've found this strange mix — old and young, urban and wild, academic and social, teacher and student — rather enriching and fascinating for all its cultural diversity.

But do the nuns know what happens here after nightfall? Each year, we are plagued by parties in the fall, and it's getting even worse as some of the party houses have moved from being amateur to professional. Students who "work" at such party houses use "valet parking" to hide cars behind trees for days, some large lawns holding as many as fifty cars parked all the way back to the trees, hidden from police and public view. The students have apps on their iPhones to pick up police scanners and also scanners to listen in on phone calls made by residents to police. As a result of technology, enterprising party houses often know when cops are on the way. They have huge bonfires burning behind storage buildings and ways of hiding in the trees behind houses so that it's impossible to tell how many people are really out there. Sometimes there are hundreds lurking in the no-man's land of the woods beneath powerlines, dozens of screaming voices calling out from the darkness of property lines and cyclone fences. Professional party houses sell alcohol and illegal substances to underage students who walk through the trees, unseen by police and residents.

The neighborhood is a war zone, divided into owners and renters, students and professors, family houses and party houses. Enemy lines are unclear, especially after 2 a.m. when the city's 311 operators stop answering phones and all reported incidents must automatically become a 911 matter.

Many of the larger homes in the neighborhood are rental properties inhabited by fraternity members and random groups of college students. The renters sometimes cause damage to the neighborhood. They live in hordes. When they run out of room to park, they kill the grass by parking in yards. Well before Halloween, the neighborhood soundtrack is random screams echoing through the night—screams of joy, screams of terror, and screams that seem to have no purpose but to call out to other screamers in gatherings behind the trees that separate the houses between Sandburg, Nash, and Ogden. Through the woods are official trails formed by sober neighbors who walk in daylight and unofficial trails formed by intoxicated students hiding from police and trespassing through lawns. They move from one house party to another, possibly to participate in a ring of illegal gambling or in search of the neighborhood "bartender."

Over the years, by studying the signs of damage and strange construction in my house, I've come to believe my house was once an illegal motel that operated in conjunction with the professional party houses on the other side of my fence. Each of my bedroom doors has a lock that fits a separate key that did not come with the house. Each of these locks resembles the sort of locks used on outside doors. After I moved in, an FBI agent came to the front door asking for a woman I had never heard of before. Someone kept calling for the woman and wouldn't believe me when I said I wasn't her and had no idea where she was.

I discovered the previous owners of my house had been scammed by their renters and had been working with the Department of Justice to resolve the issue. My house had been used in a rent-to-own scam in which the legal owners were defrauded by a "tenant" who was not even living in the house but renting the house to others and then offering to sell the house to his renters. There was a business called "Vacancy Ready" registered to this address and advertised online, although I never could tell what the business sold.

Needless to say, I knew the reasons I got the house for a song — the worst roof in the neighborhood, the worst termite damage in the crawl space, strange scratches in the hardwoods and all along the paneling in the den. Not to mention all those strange locks on the bedroom doors and the extra doors that seemed to have no real purpose but to block off all walled spaces to make more "motel" rooms. There were extra doors installed everywhere, doors between hallways making it so that each hallway could be completely enclosed and shut off from the rest of the house when all doors were locked.

College Downs has another problem — equally interesting and somewhat embarrassing — a local phenomenon known as "naked joggers." In houses on Nottoway Drive, Lewis Carroll Circle, and Sandburg Avenue, professors have reported sightings from time to time. During peak season, they stay up at all hours, staring through dark windows, searching the neighborhood for the pack of nude joggers. I'm one of them—one of the professors, that is, not one of the naked students dashing through the night, although I have secretly longed to switch teams.

Sightings of naked night-runners are reported throughout College Downs, and suddenly no one is talking about the drunk who sleeps in the woods. Because our neighborhood is so close to the University of North Carolina at Charlotte, whenever there is a problem, the university police show up at our front doors, but so far, no one has called the police about the joggers. Naked joggers are only one complaint in a long line of bizarre happenings. At one point, College Downs residents began a calling tree to report sightings in order to track the movements of naked athletes sprinting through the night.

Professors who live in College Downs are concerned and surprised by what's happening along our scenic tree-lined streets. Residents talk about the need for some sort of plan, but a plan to do what? Is this a matter for the police? Is it just some sort of practical joke, a hoax, or a prank? Even if it is a joke, does it have the potential to create serious repercussions? Wouldn't calling the police just harm the very students some of us want to protect? Would the naked joggers be forever labeled as "sex offenders" on the national registry if reported and convicted? Would any of the professors really want that?

I'm ready to ask all these questions as I walk to our neighborhood association meeting. At the same time, I wonder, what's happening to our neighborhood? Is this a teaching opportunity or a sign that our property values are soon to rapidly decline?

These are the questions on my mind as residents gather at the Advent Lutheran Church, where the neighborhood association meets twice a year. Even though some might think that we have more mundane concerns, we begin the meeting on a rather philosophical note, by asking ourselves if it's a crime for young people to jog naked in the night. And why would they want to? What is their motivation and who is being harmed and what is the risk and to whom? If a drunken man is allowed to sleep in the woods on our trail, shouldn't college students be allowed to jog naked after dark? Perhaps we are only trying to regain a sense of control by seeking the logic behind something that has no logic. Perhaps the only real reason is that there is no reason. Perhaps we are all perverts for talking about it in the first place, an older retired professor says. But I say that maybe some of us are trying to protect the neighborhood, the residents, the naked joggers, and society in general? I'm stumped by my own logic as none of us can decide exactly how we're helping anyone. In vain, we attempt to come to some sort of consensus on what to do, if anything should be done. It's still a delicate subject, especially because most of the naked joggers running through our neighborhood's streets, so far, have been female.

Sightings of naked joggers seem to increase near Lewis Carroll Circle as the parking problems on Sandburg Avenue and Bonnie Lane worsen in October, kicking off the season for football games and student parties. Eventually, the city and the police are called, to deal with the traffic issues and the parking problems, not the joggers. The naked joggers, it is decided, are a problem for the neighborhood to deal with in private; best not to get the authorities involved.

One professor, upon seeing the joggers, rushes to her car to chase the girls but loses track of them as they dart into the wooded lot. Later, the same professor thinks she recognizes the girls in daylight, fully clothed. She approaches them, accuses them, saying she recognizes them. She tries to tell them that people know what they're doing. The girls just stand still and stare at her. They then run away, laughing. Perhaps they live by their own rules, doing things their professors can only imagine. Perhaps the naked joggers are struggling to survive a season of fraternity parties the only way they know how—by doing what they are dared to do.

Neighborhoods are like people, as they have distinct characters shaped by experience and history. Of all the many neighborhoods in Charlotte, College Downs has one of the most unique histories as well as one of the most unique identity struggles. In some ways, College Downs is the best kept secret in Charlotte, or it was the best kept secret, until all the houses were recently bought up so that there is nothing left for sale in the neighborhood. Months ago, when the last houses were sold, they each got multiple competing offers within a day of listing. I'm one of the owners who came late to the game, just in time to take advantage of the dip in prices due to issues with foreclosures and economic crisis that rocked Charlotte from 2008 until 2011. There were great deals on houses everywhere just a few years ago, all over Charlotte. Now there are no houses in College Downs left to buy.

Sometimes people ask me why I chose to relocate to College Downs when there are so many neighborhoods to choose from in the Queen City. I tell them there is something electric, exciting, and indefinable that makes College Downs a special neighborhood, a sense of history and place that has evolved with the growing university just across the street.

The neighborhood's fate is directly tied to the university and always has been. Every time the university changes, the neighborhood changes, for better or for worse. In a rapidly expanding urban community with an even faster growing research institution, this means the neighborhood is always evolving like a creature adapting, struggling to survive in an ever-changing landscape, like the owl I watch each night.

AIMEE PARKISON, associate professor of English, is the creative writing coordinator at the University of North Carolina at Charlotte. She has an MFA from Cornell University. Her work has been published in literary magazines across the nation. She has received fellowships from the NC Arts Council, the Isherwood Foundation, AAS, and Writers at Work. Her most recent book is *The Innocent Party*.

The Starter House

SANDRA Y. GOVAN

"It's my house, and I live here ..."
—Diana Ross

A SIGNIFICANT PORTION of my life revolves around music. I'm usually singing something. It's only natural that when I built my first house—a colorful, compact, comfortable, and perfect-for-me house in the Grove Park subdivision of Hickory Grove—I could hear Motown's Diana Ross singing "It's My House." Her rendition became my theme song.

Those Ashford and Simpson lyrics assert, "It's my house, and I live here ... There's my chair, I put it there." Those lines worked for me. They were my declaration of defiance. My affirmation of self, my certainty that, as they say these days, "I got this." Diana's voice evoked all that roiled within me when I purchased my little starter house, a house that was, as Marvin Gaye and Tammi Terrell sang, "all I need to get by."

You would not think that in 1984 a brand new assistant professor at the University of North Carolina at Charlotte would make such a big deal over buying a house. But that was just it. I was brand new—to the university and to the community. I'd only been on the job a year. Furthermore, I had no credit history in North Carolina. No bank would give me a loan.

Add to those indignities the sage, unsolicited advice of my mother back in Chicago who said, "Sweetie, why don't you *wait* and see if you get tenure *before* you buy a house?" To dampen the heat Mama undoubtedly felt radiating up the phone line, she added, "If you wait, I'll help with the down payment; I'll pay the closing costs too."

Bribery! No other word for it. Black mothers have a legendary history of trying to protect their children from all conceivable harm, I know, but Jesus! I was grown! Most certainly grown enough in 1984 to handle the rent-or-buy decision by myself. Still seething from that talk, I immediately dialed Mary Harper, my friend in the English department who had raised three daughters. She also served as my surrogate mother.

"What's *wrong* with you Black mamas?"

"What Sarah do to you now?"

"Nothing," I spluttered. "She just thinks I still don't have no sense."

"Well," Mary laughed, "you only cussing me, because you can't cuss your mama." As I cooled, we talked about the weirdness of mothers who throw cold water, or what they think of as seasoned reason, on their children's dreams.

I had moved to Charlotte from Lexington, Kentucky, where I'd taught for three years in the University of Kentucky English Department. There, I'd rented a two-story duplex—my first house after grad school. It was nice. But accessible it was not. And accessibility was important. When the invitation to move to Charlotte came, I accepted without regret.

That began my way overextended, terribly overcommitted, and woefully underpaid provisional period as an assistant professor. While Mama cautioned me to "sit tight until you get tenure," there was no guarantee, no carved-in-stone assurance that what she wanted would happen unless I worked at it. Sitting tight comfortably for the next several years while the sometimes-adversarial academic process played out was not going to be easy without a comfortable place to sit. Besides, I'd taken that leap of faith that says, "I've come too far from where I started from." While the road most decidedly would not be easy, I recognized, somewhat cynically to be sure, that politically I came as a triple treat for the university — a talented Black *woman* with a disability. My Leo ego said, "They hired you; do the work really well and they cannot deny you." I just needed to find a good place to do that work.

During the first year when I rented a duplex in East Charlotte's Shannon Park area, I became friends with Shirley Harris and Eloise Carter, two Black women who lived near my place. They were single and home-owners. By example, they showed me that it was possible for a woman, living on just a bit more than a shoestring, to not only own a home but to take care of one as well. Their down-to-earth courage convinced me that I, too, could become a homeowner.

Various realtors, who showed me most of Charlotte, talked to me about a "starter house." A starter house. What a strange concept. I'd never heard tell of such a place. The very idea seemed utterly foreign. Where I came from, and based on my folks' Chicago experience — indeed, most of my home neighborhood's experience — when you bought a home, you stayed in it for *life*. But in Charlotte, it was different — a house got you started on the road to bigger, better houses.

I wanted my starter house to be designed to help meet certain physi-cal challenges I knew were coming. A few years earlier, a Kentucky doctor had given me notice when he announced calmly, "You have epiphyseal dys-plasia." Then he predicted, "Where all the long bones are joined, your joints will disintegrate over time."

Forewarned is forearmed. I knew I needed a special place, an *accessible* place. But Charlotte realtors didn't seem to think it really mattered whether the houses they showed me met any of my expressed needs — well built, no steps, gas heat, spacious but manageable, avoidance of I-85 but proximity to the university — because, they said, "You'll just move in a few years."

After viewing all manner of distressingly unsuitable dwellings—too big, too small, too far from anything, totally inaccessible, or major fixer-uppers with cracks running from the foundation through the walls—I began shopping around alone. I found a new development in Grove Park. The site drawing or "elevation" that the developer showed me depicted a house that looked to me like a Goldilocks house with everything "just right."

The finished product proved true to the rendering. The house had a spacious kitchen that looked like one of those television-commercial kitchens where the counter surfaces nearly go wall to wall, and the floor had sufficient space not just to mop, but to skate across (if one could skate)! The kitchen's huge picture window looked out on the front yard.

Then there were the cabinets! My mother, who immediately retreated from her "you-don't-need-no-house" stance once she saw all that cabinet space, loved it. (Mama was also extraordinarily fond of the linen closet; every time she came to visit, she made it her business to *help* me straighten it.) And Misty Gilead Govan, who had traveled with me from Kentucky, thoroughly enjoyed leaping from countertop to refrigerator top to cabinet top. There, resting upon her grand new perch, she would steadily lick a black and white paw while peering down, surveying her terrain from the high ground. It was as if she prayed for some misguided field mouse to wander in from the wilderness right into her snare. Ever hopeful, she continually glanced through the screened back door, ready to pounce.

It was very different having a kitchen with that Janus quality to it—I could either look out the back door to the yard or I could sit facing that front window and comfortably watch the world of the cul-de-sac. The morning sun lit that room so brightly because I'd painted it sunshine yellow. Without question the kitchen remained the cheeriest space to sit and read after breakfast, or sit and daydream after lunch, or sit and talk following dinner.

Where some new homes on the block were wood frame, decorated in optimistic greens, blues, or yellows, my starter house wore a reddish brick exterior on three sides and orange melon-painted compressed wood on the back. The shutters were a deeper warm red—not a garish blood red, but a red that proclaimed, "Color can be your key to looking good." I'd seen that headline in the *Charlotte Observer*, clipped it, and kept it taped to my office door at the university for years, enjoying its subtlety. Set against the dark green foliage of the trees in my yard, the brand new Casa Govan looked good. Without bending to bland browns or neutral naturals, the house announced it fit the neighborhood yet it had its own piquant vibrancy.

Inside, down the wider-than-average hallway leading from the kitchen, there were two east-facing bedrooms that caught morning light. The living room sat across the hallway and doubled as my music room, complete with a stereo system and paintings depicting jazz musicians. It had a fireplace, with two windows looking out to a yard framed by trees.

The first bedroom down that hallway was my guestroom; the second, my study. I hired Willie Goodman, a new friend who doubled as a handyman I'd met through Shirley and Eloise, to construct built-in bookcases.

Across from the study, down a short hallway, past the hall bathroom (Misty's bath, complete with litter box) sat the Mistress Suite. This bedroom fit me perfectly! There were two huge closets—a His and a Hers, or more appropriately, Spring and Fall wardrobe-holders. A window at one end of the room and two more beside the head of the bed filled the room with light. A few steps from the nightstand stood the accompanying compact bathroom—the Mistress Bath.

Talk about joy! The snug bathroom not only held an accessible or "comfort height" throne but had a true walk-in shower with only one slight step! Most importantly, the shower had grab-bars, those securely inserted vertical and horizontal safety-bars all Baby Boomers should install now! The windows were not fussy; I covered them with mini-blinds.

Willie, who created my bookcases, also built a raised flower box near the front entry and a solid, spacious, beautiful railed deck with built-in benches and tables in the rear of the house. Sadly, he was killed while driving to Charlotte from Rock Hill. The whole of East Charlotte mourned.

This soft-spoken midnight gift of a man did so much for all of us—from tax preparation to auto repair to plumbing. At his funeral I watched grown men sob into hand towels and women wail into wads of tissue.

But let me be clear. It was not just the new house I loved; indeed, I loved the whole neighborhood, which was in fact only a few miles from where I had started my Charlotte life. I could be at Shirley's or Eloise's home in five minutes or so.

As I said, my starter house was located in Grove Park. The area had once been farmland (hence my address: "Farmgate" Drive) on the eastern edge of Charlotte. My house bordered land owned by Hickory Grove Presbyterian Church, which then sat on Newell-Hickory Grove Road, a street that, with several name changes, ran from Independence past UNC-Charlotte.

The Charlotte Observer's "Mecklenburg Neighbors" described both the street and neighborhood in the early 1980s as booming. A consequence of the "New Hickory Grove" was dramatically increased traffic. *The Observer* reported, "Nearly 20,000 cars a day flow down Newell-Hickory Grove and Delta roads, already a major link between south Charlotte and the UNCC area and the future path of the Harris Boulevard Extension"—an artery those of us still living here know as East W.T. Harris Boulevard. Traffic or no, Hickory Grove managed to retain its identity, and still holds an annual Fourth of July parade where sections of the road are blocked off and adults take their children and lawn chairs to watch the spectacle.

Until about 1987, when I drove from my Grove Park homestead each day to teach, I passed Holstein cows, wonder of wonders to a city girl, still grazing on pasture land, munching, mooing, and watching the cars cruise by!

Not only was my Farmgate house accessible, so was easy shopping. Folks in East Charlotte did not have to travel across town to SouthPark to go to the mall. We could shop at Eastland Mall. Charlottean Deborah McLendon and I recently shared fond memories of the old Eastland, now rubble.

It had big department stores, as well as a wonderful mix of smaller shops. I bought my everyday china from Ivey's, which later became Dillard's; I still use that set every morning because the primary colors rimming each dish lift my spirits.

It is worth noting that Eastland featured an ice skating arena. When you tired of shopping, you could watch the skillful glide across the ice — children and adults racing, kids chasing each other despite slipping or falling, and graceful young women pirouetting as if practicing for a spectacular career.

At one time, the easily accessible Eastland served as the cultural mecca for much of Charlotte. People met for meals or movies; young people courted; older folk walked the mall's long corridors and shopped. But eventually the wealthy, and high-end development with them, moved. To the south, SouthPark Mall expanded. To the north, Northlake and Concord Mills got bigger and fancier. Eastland fell out of favor.

Grove Park, not the university, became the center of my community. In 1984, my first year in the starter house, I joined the Big Brothers/Big Sisters organization. Florence, the twelve-year-old Little Sister I was matched with, came to my house almost every weekend that year. Though we were about the same height, we were opposites attracting in every other measure. She was shy and withdrawn; I could and would talk to everybody.

Florence and I put up my very first Christmas tree and, of course, decorated it. We shopped together; we cooked together. I showed her how to make pancakes and waffles from scratch in my sunny kitchen; we also cooked my favorite Girl Scout breakfast from my youth, Toads-in-a-Hole (an egg dropped into the cut-out hole in a slice of buttered bread browned in a skillet, then served with a jam-covered round cut-out "cap" topping the toad in its hole!). Florence helped me clean the house and thereby earned her allowance; I went to seventh grade track meets and school programs. When she turned thirteen, along with Miss

Midori (the daughter of a colleague), we held a "Crossing of the Bar" or a "Rites of Womanhood" initiation ceremony. We had popcorn nights and movie nights — "Who you gonna call? Ghostbusters!" We danced through the house to the film's funky beat or Prince's "Purple Rain" or Michael Jackson's "Thriller." Sometimes the three of us, with other friends tagging along, just hung out in my living room.

The older part of Grove Park was an established neighborhood with clear boundaries. The neighborhood was framed by East W.T. Harris Boulevard, Robinson Church Road, and meandering Linda Lake Drive, which coiled around until it met Robinson Church. Williams Road ran between Harris and Linda Lake. And Farmgate, my street, connected to Williams. I came to know those streets intimately because I walked them, first on crutches and then on a cane, during the summer of 1985, the year of my first hip-replacement surgery.

The surgery took place at what was then Charlotte Orthopedic Hospital. My orthopedist performed, under some pressure from me, a total bilateral hip replacement. That is, he operated on both hips within a week of each other.

Because I had no family in the Carolinas, my mother, my father, my brother, and my closest childhood girlfriend, Stella, came to Charlotte in shifts to see about me. Daddy had retired but Mama still worked. So he came for the operation; then Mama arrived after and he ferried her around. They stayed at Casa Govan and took care of Misty the cat, with Daddy bringing home most of my hospital lunch for her.

When Mama returned to Chicago, Daddy would come visit a few hours each day to meet my Charlotte friends and newly acquired relatives like Cousin James who popped by regularly. Afterwards, he would go hit a few balls at the now-defunct public golf course on the Plaza and Eastway Drive. For sustenance, my friends and colleagues played commando, sneaking past hospital guards with contraband — hotdogs, cheeseburgers, French

151

fries, hot breakfast biscuits—foods they knew I liked. One raider even graciously brought me Maker's Mark; I took a tiny hit to show appreciation.

Most of my hospital facetime was spent in relentless exercise. Mama initially sat with me during the roughest exercise routines, encouraging me to hold on, do my best, all the usual moral support clichés. My goal was to be back at Farmgate and walking through the neighborhood.

Finally, after almost a month in Orthopedic, the hospital kicked me out, saying if I could climb their practice stairs on crutches, then roll around the hospital playing in the wheelchair all night, I could do my adduction and abduction exercises at home. That began the long road to recovery, largely with the help of friends, family, and the home PTs who came biweekly to test my strength and my nerves.

I remember lying on my bed in the Mistress Suite, repeatedly doing leg lifts, using a royal blue leg-puller toy to get my leg started in the lifting motion. Within a week I put the device aside to spare myself the pain of becoming dependent on it. I remember dangling a foot over the bed's edge, then struggling to "lift from the hip" to get the thigh muscles restarted and that foot back up on the bed. Another medical device, a triangle practice bar installed over my bed, helped me pull myself up enough so Daddy could prop pillows behind me when I was still eating in my room.

By the time Daddy left, I was doing pretty well, except that I'd lost more weight. Daddy's concept of a good meal, beyond his wonderful breakfasts, was limited. He broiled T-bones and fixed a god-awful salad with bananas, apples, *and onions* on a thick bed of iceberg lettuce. Don't get me wrong. I loved my daddy. In fact, because he was a natural storyteller, I learned a lot about his painful childhood. But, damn, *banana and onion?* I simply could not eat another one of his "Duke's Mixtures," another of his strange concoctions he'd had me taste as a child.

The arrival of Stella, my childhood friend, proved a welcome relief. Taking me outside to sit in a lawn chair she'd placed on the stoop, Stella admonished me to "just breathe." She wanted me to "take in the fresh air" and watch the vinca grow that she'd planted in Willie's flower box. "Yvonne," she said, "you've been in the house too long. And all you do is work. You walk down the block and back; then down the block again and back. Sit a minute."

I had my own routine I established to quickly regain what mobility I could.

Almost every visitor that summer—Daddy, Stella, my brother, or friends—walked down Farmgate with me. Even Misty sometimes accompanied me, scooting under parked cars, scurrying across open spaces, and keeping an eye peeled for unleashed dogs or trees to climb. Once she got careless; a dog did attack but could not catch her as, quoting my daddy, "up that tree she had business!"

Each day, twice a day, I walked. Down the flat driveway; out to the street; down to that next mailbox. Did I mention that Farmgate had no sidewalks? No sidewalks until I hit Williams Road. To be truthful, I didn't obey all the rules for walkers. I walked *with* traffic rather than *against* it. Neighbors got accustomed to seeing me and often came outside to cheer me on.

By the time Stella returned to her world and my brother arrived in mine, I could almost walk to Williams. My brother's visit to Casa Govan changed the course of my exercise routine. It was a hot, *hot*, summer, and I was staying indoors more to exercise. My brother did not treat me as "the delicate shut-in." He actually made being on crutches fun—he'd throw a couch pillow at me, force me to chase him around the living room and down the hall as payback for tossing the pillow in the first place! It was as if I was eight and he was ten, and he'd hit me and forced me to run after him to retaliate. Now he had me careening around the house like I was starring in some jungle movie, using my crutches to jump rivers. Like when we were children, he stayed just beyond my punching range. But with the extended reach of crutches, I did get to pop him a few times.

By the time he left, I was well on my way to moving down Williams Road. My new goal was to go all the way to Linda Lake Drive, one mailbox at a time. I was building endurance. I finally reached it one sultry September afternoon — all the way down to gaze upon peaceful, little Linda Lake. Victory!

Having made my goal, I began to climb back uphill when disaster struck. Yep. Unmitigated disaster. The screw on my left crutch fell out on the street. The crutch came apart. I did not fall, but now the goal was to get all the way back home on one crutch. Normally, there would be traffic, and somebody would stop and give me a ride. What motorist wouldn't stop for a woman using one crutch and carrying a second in the same hand — a skill taught by all those Physical Terrorists? But that last hot day of summer, there was no traffic, nobody working in a yard, no one out pruning shrubs. There was nothing to it but do it. So up the hill I climbed.

By the time I reached Farmgate, I was exhausted. By the time I reached my house, I was way past exhaustion and in total wipe-out. But I'd done it. Made it all the way back to my house.

Like anyone else who has ever owned and loved a first home, I have many fond memories of it — the meals served there, like the first real Thanksgiving when friends from Philadelphia brought with them the turkey, dressing, and veggies, while I baked all the desserts. And the tale of the perfectly seasoned *roast beef* I'd carefully placed in the oven for my first romantic dinner there that came out of the oven when my company arrived as *roast pork*. More memories involve friends who visited, parties held. But my strongest memories are of my mother, her recognition that it *was* my house, not hers. I built it. I owned it. I designed its welcoming warmth.

And that end-of-the-hallway linen closet my mother loved so much? On her last visit to the Farmgate house, she gathered what ebbing strength she had left and took as her mission straightening that closet one last time.

I lived in my little Farmgate starter house far longer than any of the realtors expected. It's likely I would have remained there except that one bright morning I awoke with the startling thought, *My next house will be my Dream House.* Then I started to build my second home.

A member of the Wintergreen Women Writers' Collective and professor emerita from the University of North Carolina at Charlotte, **SANDRA Y. GOVAN** is enjoying retirement. She lectures for the North Carolina Humanities Council and occasionally teaches African American Literature at UNC-Charlotte. When possible, she attends exercise classes, travels, participates in professional activities, and really enjoys honing her creative abilities.

Eastland's Child

AMY HALLMAN

WITH ALL THE CONTROVERSY Eastland Mall stirred up in Charlotte in the first months of 2014, one would have thought the mall was still up and running. Or at least standing. But the city's most newsworthy mall had in fact been reduced to mounds of recyclable material, a muddled field of dreams.

In 2010, Eastland fell silent; its owner pulled the plug, choosing fore-closure over salvation. A second corporation came to the rescue, assuring Charlotteans of a Christmas renaissance in 2011. The city held its collective breath, though Christmas didn't come to Eastland that year. Its last two owners hailed from halfway across the country, boasting millions of elabo-rately developed real estate square footage. Both fulfilled an out-of-sight/ out-of-mind prophecy: Their most impressive works are located within driving distances of their corporate offices. Both eventually dumped East-land Mall.

The following summer, the city of Charlotte became the sole owner of the entire eighty-acre parcel, hoping to facilitate a potential sale to a developer. Again, the community crossed its fingers. After all, multiple film companies showed interest in developing a studio there. If this could happen, then hotels and other businesses would surely follow. The traffic flow, the mall's lifeblood, could be restored.

Only ten short months after voting to purchase the property, the city council denied the once-touted "futuristic" mall its last stay of execution. In a 10 to 1 vote, the council agreed to pay almost $1 million to raze the nearly forty-year-old structure.

For months after that landmark decision (no pun intended), I avoided the demolition's newspaper and television coverage. All this business about tearing something down just didn't reconcile with all that Eastland had once built.

On the surface, Eastland was a place you could drop off your teens, purchase add-a-beads for your coveted necklace, or buy the latest Beastie Boys cassette. It was a place where girls of all ages could dream of Prince Charming amid Poffy Girls' walls of taffeta and tulle in every color. On another level, this microcosm of diversity and accession was enticingly unlike my own, affording me greater treasures than any I could have bought.

Though it opened in 1975, at the cusp of the city's transition from Old South to New, my first complete memory of Eastland dates back to 1980: My mother kept me out of school to celebrate "my womanhood" by going shopping. Such trips quickly became a mother-daughter tradition to celebrate any event or to lessen a disappointment; there was no occasion that it couldn't make better. Our favorite time to go to Eastland was Christmas Eve to watch panicked last-minute shoppers. We took a certain perverse pleasure in this annual ritual that involved eating giant slices of Tasos' pepperoni pizza and giggling a lot of "bless their hearts" for those for whom closing time was akin to the death knell.

We probably visited the mall every other week, creating a code for this bonding time: "Bong bong." Even my dad knew where we were going when my mom melodiously sang, "Bong bong!" At that time, Belk used that ringtone to signal an impending announcement. It wasn't the cacophonic antitheft alarm often used today, but the pleasant Siren song of our happy place.

Lunches at Tuesday's (later Annabelle's) signaled a special occasion, marked by French onion soup and girl talk. It was here that I learned just why my mom resented living in my great-grandparents' old house. Unlike me, Mom didn't go into great detail or explanation; she has always been the great protector of what's-bottled-inside. Guarding her deepest thoughts, she preferred to lead me with absolutes. "You will not. . . ." There was no "or else." There was no consequence because that was all. The end. Our world was fantastic. I didn't know anything else. But I suspected.

In an era before the Internet or cell phones, and with very little cable television, Eastland Mall represented the whole world. We could stroll all day, making neither heads nor tails of anything in particular and no one would care. That was part of the allure for my mom. No one could keep a detailed account of her time management or her conversations.

While Charlotte's Uptown skyline began to reflect its aspirations to become a banking powerhouse, "the city that made integration work" (stated so often no one remembers who first said this) would soon elect its first African American mayor. Eastland, too, seemed a jewel in the Queen City's crown in every way.

Over the years, Eastland's décor became outdated, but in the moment we called it tradition. And tradition in the South wasn't something you messed with. The stores all sold current clothing and modern designs, so the giant glass and chrome globe lights (circa 1975) were simply a part of the Eastland charm. If you even noticed them at all, you didn't think about their datedness. Besides, there was always magic on that ice skating rink. Who needed to be surrounded by the latest architectural features to be entranced by the skaters: students taking lessons, competitive athletes in training, or kids out there playing a frosty version of bumper cars. Their giggles amid the sprays of ice from skate blades floated up and carried you away.

Eastland offered an escape from my rural north Mecklenburg neighborhood and its narrow view of the world. Charlotte's school bussing system, which had been around for nearly two decades by then, still seemed to engender as much resentment as it did support. One Monday morning, a popular football player stopped me in the hall to question me about dancing "with the wrong color" at a weekend party. By high school, I felt increasingly alienated from the world that was supposed to be home.

Not unlike my mother, I found Eastland to be a refuge. But I found that I craved the culture and experience it offered rather than just the escape, even if I was quite content to learn vicariously. My friends didn't live where I lived, and it dawned on me that maybe I was the one living in the wrong place. This education wasn't even limited to textbooks — my eleventh grade English teacher never used the word *adultery* during our entire study of *The Scarlet Letter*. In a world in which we couldn't talk about what Hester Prynne was up to, Toni Morrison and Alice Walker didn't exist.

The summer before I officially became a college English major, I immersed myself in less lofty pursuits — girlfriends, Gap jeans, and George Thorogood music blasting on my boom box. What better way to honor this right of passage than to spend more time — and to get paid — at Eastland!

The mall was a thirty-minute drive from our house; so my $4.50-an-hour summer sales job hardly allowed me to break even. But this girl was paid in other riches: clothes. The boxy red and orange color blocks, thick-cabled sweaters, and leggings were the style! The forest green and brown paneled blazer complemented the suede aubergine ankle boots. We called them Prince boots because they looked like something his Purple Highness himself might wear. At Paul Harris, my second job at the mall, associates relished the monthly sales competitions — who didn't want the prize of hundreds of dollars in clothing in addition to our 40 percent discount? Unbeknownst to us, the national chain was staving off bankruptcy, but we were too busy turning an oversized sweater into a sassy dress with a colorful pair of tights. Bliss!

Although I would graduate from NC State, everything I knew was in Charlotte: my friends, my family, my interests. By my senior year, I went to classes Tuesday through Thursday and headed back for the weekend in the Queen City, where I always felt more regal anyway.

Even though I still have bouts of euphoric fashion memories, Eastland for me will always be about the people. While on a lunch break from my first job in another store, I made the fortuitous left turn into Paul Harris and asked for an application, looking for more hours. The manager, Diann, seated on the floor and building a display, turned and looked me up and down without apology. It probably helped that I was wearing one of their current Pasta trends. She hired me. I spent the next two years there, making love-you-for-life friends: Tammy, Lisa, and Diann. In fact, later I followed Diann to a different store and a different mall, a path on which I learned how to make changes that are in my best interest, and not necessarily in my heart—a skill that wasn't innate or even encouraged where I came from. That woman was tenacity and love all rolled into one spitfire, petite package. Even Mom loved Diann—and she entrusted her to manage me however she saw fit.

One Christmas season, Diann taught me my first substantial service lesson. During a particularly heavy return period, I was working the register when a customer brought back Santa's sack full of clothes, though she had no receipt. She insisted the receipt was in the bag she'd handed to me to empty. Though I repeatedly practiced my best empathetic voice and picked up each clothing item in case the receipt would materialize from its folds, the customer would only repeat, "The receipt is in the bag," as if pleading the Fifth. Frazzled by the impasse, I took the paper bag, turned it upside down, and shook it in mock-support. 'Tis the season to return! I was out of polite conversation. But Diann, watching all this unfold, gracefully swept in and ushered me to "cover the front of the store," so she could "take care of this customer." She probably wanted to kill me; but Diann had an endearing way of building you up (or tearing you down first) that incited loyalty and respect. It was a model I carried with me through my teaching career:

If you're going to challenge someone to think, first you have to establish acceptance and respect. This was a far cry from my experiences at home: *Shut your mouth and don't let anyone see you with them.*

Diann also taught me that style may be acceptably risky but need not be trashy. Nor oppressive. If I really wanted to rock that spandex LBD (and what twenty-year-old didn't?), I had to forego the bra. She relieved me of it in one swift move: Standing in the middle of Plum Crazy on Tyvola Road, just before a Peace & Love concert, she pulled my bra out from under my dress, stuffed it in her purse, and said, "That's better." She was ahead of her time, improving fashion's sightlines — without the benefit of Spanx!

In 1990, not all high-end clothing stores were a SouthPark exclusive: Today, I still have several pairs of designer boots from Leather 'N Wood, located near the ice rink, that look as current and fun as the day I bought them. Their cost, then comparable to rent. . . but twenty years later, people unreservedly compliment the red cowboy boots I bought at Eastland Mall. Looking at me as if I'd said they had been tucked away with the lost ark, they say, "You did *not!*" How could something from Eastland last long enough to be vintage? How could anything from that mall have endured? And while that's not my story of Eastland, unfortunately that's how the official story will go.

The signs were there by the early 2000s when outlet stores replaced original anchors. Once, Eastland's three-screen movie theater heralded great success with Midnight Movies, but competition came from the Regency Theater's $1 first-run movies just down Albemarle Road; and the bright and shiny University Place cineplex near UNC-Charlotte was much closer for my friends to watch movies, walk around its little lake, and still make curfew. In 2005, a shooting inside Eastland branded the mall as dangerous; a second shooting the following year dashed any hopes of recovery.

In contrast, the culture at *my* Eastland seemed safe and accepting and steadfast. It was a time when Carrot Top was still Scott — a couple of years before he achieved *Tonight Show* recognition — and WWE's Tatanka, still known only as Chris, had just begun his ascension to wrestling super-stardom, following the hyperbolic road that Ric Flair had paved through Charlotte. Eastland was the first place I ever saw the Charlotte Hornets' purple and teal emblazoned on hats and shirts. The colors seemed to proclaim, *We're all on the same team.* It didn't matter if you lived on the east side or the west or if you drove in from the north or the south—Charlotteans from all walks of life came to Eastland to shop and to play.

And so it was, for quite a few years—a touchstone—culturally and socially . . . and materially.

For better or worse, we live in a culture of expendability—*If you don't like it, replace it.* For example, in 1988, CityFair opened in the heart of Uptown and was razed only eleven years later to make way for the Hearst Tower. In fact, Emporis.com reports at least seventeen central Charlotte buildings, some dating to the late 1800s, have been demolished recently. Most have been replaced with today's banking high-rises or parking lots. Uptown's transformation has slowly rippled throughout Charlotte.

The inundation of apartment complexes created a pseudo-revitaliza-tion around the mall. The construction looked good initially—everything new, new, new, including the people. *If you build it, they will come.* But the transient nature of these rental properties could not sustain Eastland, espe-cially without its own reformation. Soon, strip malls popped up, with pawn shops, check-cashing storefronts, and dollar stores. There was little or no pedestrian traffic—save the occasional life-threatening sprint across four-lane roads. Forget a bicycle.

While SouthPark has undergone extensive renovations throughout the years, Eastland did little more than freshen up the paint and replace floor treatments. A 2013 Charlotte-Mecklenburg Historic Landmark Commis-sion report suggests that Belk's larger scale renovation of its SouthPark store in the late Eighties signaled the beginning of the end for Eastland. It wasn't deliberate. In fact, it seemed to happen while no one was look-ing. While the city celebrated abounding progress in the north and south, the blood loss from its city's heart grew too great for Eastland to survive.

When I reminisce about Eastland, it's impossible to separate the build-ing—its location, materials, and architectural features, or its sights, smells, sounds, and tastes—from the guts of it. I can't do it. Eastland Mall's legacy is not summarized in a newspaper report about fewer sales and antiquated design. Eastland Mall was an anachronism of culture and equality that helped me to redefine my own boundaries, create my own identity.

All those years my mom took me to Eastland to prepare me for a very particular path she had all picked out for me. By junior high, I realized just how narrow that path was. She only meant to walk me straight down the middle of the road, not too far right, and certainly not too far left; but she couldn't accept my values as readily as she expected me to accept hers. Things change sometimes for the better, and sometimes not; and some-times we mistake one for the other.

Almost in complement to her, though, Eastland taught me something else, something she perhaps didn't yet know herself: Without a willingness to reflect and change, you will suffocate. Without growth, your efforts are in vain.

Despite its extinction, Eastland will always be more valuable than the sum of its recycled and repurposed parts. Our society tends to recognize progress only if it agrees with the outcome. But maybe progress sometimes includes an ending. It may not be the outcome we want or the one we necessarily see coming, but the end of one extraordinary era does not have to lessen the value of its existence or its inspiration.

AMY HALLMAN has lived in north Mecklenburg County since she was a year old. She taught high school English, journalism, and creative writing in and around Charlotte for nine-teen years. She is the editor of *Lake Norman Woman Magazine*.

Rooted

VIRGINIA BROWN

AN OLD WILLOW OAK stands alone on the perimeter of a newly razed lot in South End. It's taller than most of the other trees around. Its trunk, shooting up about fifty feet, is dotted with the scars of lost branches. It's probably the oldest thing remaining on the street, and it looks slightly stressed out. Nearly half of its lush canopy is gone, unevenly hacked to make room for drooping power lines. It's not perfect, but it's still standing.

The buildings that stood here are gone, making way for new condos. Snapped window frames and cinder blocks, now crumbled to near dust, form harsh dunes in the sad space. Signs that read *Demolition Experts* drape a ratty chain-link fence that surrounds a construction claw powered by a machine with tank-like wheels. Someone could have started a family business here. A baby might have learned to walk inside. Still the buildings came down. But the oak stands.

In Charlotte, our trees give us a sense of place. Like pickles on hot dogs in Chicago. Or music in Memphis. Some of our trees have been around for more than 150 years, longer than the buildings in our pop-up skyline and much longer than any of us.

This isn't by accident. We coexist with trees in an urban forest that is the product of the careful planning of those who came before us — and the protection of those who still care. The system isn't perfect. But we try. We try because the trees have become part of who we are. Charlotte's national identity might be a blend of North meets South, with big banks and race cars sprinkled in. But our soul is in the trees.

Patrick George fights for the trees. He grew up in the Starmount neighborhood off South Boulevard at a time before much of anything had developed, before takeout Chinese joints and dry cleaners dominated strip malls. And well before the light rail.

When school let out in the afternoons, Patrick explored the woods behind his house. A wooded area and Little Sugar Creek converged into the perfect place for a kid's imagination. One day, when he was twelve years old, Patrick ran out to find nothing there. His trees were gone. "I was devastated," he says. "I ran home and asked my parents what happened, and my mom told me that the power company had gone in and chopped them all down," he says, eyes cast on the floor, as if reflecting on old friends.

The street names in Starmount today — Wrentree Drive, Woodstream Drive, Oakstone Place, Mapleridge Drive — serve as reminders, like names carved into the planks of roadside picnic tables. Trees were here.

Patrick is middle-aged now, bearded and balding only on top. Having protected and groomed our trees for more than thirty years, he's the closest thing Charlotte has to the Lorax. If you didn't know he was a tree guy, you might mistake him for a park ranger. Or a mountain climber. He's fit and tan, and most days he wears olive-colored, Patagonia-style pants, the kind with hooks and loops and all sorts of contraptions. Outside his office is a sculpture made of parts of a willow oak that reads *ROOTS*.

Patrick is the founder of Heartwood Tree Service, a tree-care company with the tagline "Helping trees outlive people since 1979." He's probably spent more time with bark and branches than he's spent with humans.

And he knows more about trees than most people do too. "I've been asked to sit on the panels and the councils and all that, but I prefer to fight," he says. "I like to fight for the trees."

In 2005, the city planned to chop down the cherry trees that line Little Sugar Creek in Freedom Park. The Yoshino cherries, some of the first to flower in spring, are icons of the historic park. Charlotteans were livid. After the *Charlotte Observer* ran a few stories about the local fury, Patrick decided to get involved. A city official had considered the trees diseased and at the end of their lives, but Patrick and his team climbed the cherries, shortened some of the horizontal limbs, then had a 200-pound man climb out on each to show they were safe for children. Now he's responsible for their upkeep. He won the fight.

Of course, he can't save every tree. When a tree dies or becomes infected, or when an insistent client requests it, he'll cut one down. And when he does, he holds a funeral. "Trees have a history. Many of them have been there longer than the houses," he says, "so when a homeowner wants me to cut one down—one that's healthy—I always tell them, 'Give it a year. Live with a tree through all four seasons; then decide.'"

Patrick stands at one end of a long line of locals who have invested in the city's trees. A little more than a century ago, John Myers owned a nearly treeless cotton field across from today's Manor Theatre on Providence Road. He planted rows of trees and filled the front yard of this "country home" with flowers and shrubs. Locals started calling it "Myers Park." When Myers decided to turn his farm into a suburb for those wealthy enough to have two homes, one in the city and one in the country, he called on John Nolen.

Known for planning cities from San Diego to Savannah, Nolen uprooted hundreds of small trees from more rural areas—today's Cotswold and Oakhurst—and hauled them to the new suburb in the backs of pickup trucks. He ignored the popular grid plans of the time and went well beyond the average planner, naming the specific trees and flowers to be planted.

Not everyone has been as thoughtful. Around the same time Nolen was planning and planting in Myers Park, Charlotte was growing at an unruly pace. The electric trolley and birth of Dilworth meant the start of a suburban boom. The Norfolk & Southern Railway arrived a couple of years later, bringing more people, more growth.

Progress has always been at the forefront of the city's struggle to protect trees. Charles Bland, Charlotte's mayor from 1911 to 1915, is known for his support of "The Great White Way," a project led by James B. Duke and the Southern Power Company, now Duke Energy. Brilliant streetlamps, all in a row along Tryon Street, would replace the trees and mimic that of New York City in a sort of B-list Broadway. A visiting landscape architect, appropriately named Paul B. Forest, protested the Way, calling it "the grossest error." But in the winter of 1912, the trees along Tryon came down.

Today, rows of healthy trees intertwine with streetlights along East Bland Street in South End. And Myers Park is the city's most beautiful neighborhood, shaded and coveted.

Trees are the life of Charlotte's party. One of the first things out-of-towners notice about the city is how green it is—how many trees we have. When our families and friends visit, we can't wait to show off Queens Road West and tunnel through its cathedral canopy. We have nearly forty miles of developed greenway that, without trees, would be a frying pan in the summer. There's a cell-phone tower behind the Harris YMCA designed to look like a tree. And in our airport, inside the terminal, are two rows of Bradford pears.

Our visitor center lists a horse-drawn carriage tour through Fourth Ward's tree canopy as one of 101 fun things to do in Charlotte. And six years ago, when *CNN Money* ranked the top 100 cities to live in and launch a business, Charlotte ranked eighth. The reasons? "This national financial hub is home to big names like Wachovia and Bank of America, but the oak-tree-lined city is also a great place to launch and grow a small business." Trees made the opening line.

According to a "tree inventory" taken by American Forests, the oldest nonprofit tree conservancy in the country, Charlotte has 215 species of trees. Not surprisingly, willow oaks and crepe myrtles are found most often. We have an estimated 180,000 street trees growing between the sidewalks and curbs. And our urban canopy covers about 47 percent of the city.

But we don't just surround ourselves with trees; we plan events around them. Each year, the Charlotte Arborists Association, a nonprofit that meets bimonthly to talk trees, sponsors a Tree Climbing Competition in Freedom Park. Fifty-one climbers attended in 2013, and the winner for the men, Cormac Nagan, owns Aerial Tree Works in Durham—two-and-a-half hours away.

We have fun with our trees and work hard to keep them around. City arborist Don McSween says Charlotte has the highest canopy tree cover of any major city in the nation. For every seven Charlotteans, there's one public tree. And American Forests named Charlotte one of the ten best cities for urban forests, a distinction we share with notably lush cities like Portland and Seattle.

It takes a lot of effort to maintain that distinction. Back in 1974, Charlotte hired a city arborist, responsible for managing the street-tree program and tracking each tree's location, species, age, and condition. McSween and his staff now make up the twelve-member Charlotte Tree Advisory Commission. Our tree ordinance, established in 1978, requires developers to maintain 10 percent of the trees found on each lot. It's set up to protect "heritage" trees, like the trees listed on the state or national champion lists, and "specimen" trees, impressive examples of particular species.

We live in one of the top ten fastest-growing areas in the nation. From 1985 to 2008, strip malls surged, main drags were widened, and parking lots popped up everywhere. The city's population grew by 39 percent.

Development led to the loss of nearly half of our trees. To avoid that kind of crushing loss in the future, the Charlotte City Council set a goal in 2011 to increase the tree canopy to 50 percent shade coverage by 2050. And development aside, some of the major parts of the canopy—like many of the trees in Myers Park—are getting old and may fall soon. It's a lofty goal if the population continues to grow at the rate it has over the past few decades. More people mean more roads, more lot-clearing for more P.F. Chang's and malls.

To meet the goal, we'll have to plant 15,000 trees each year in addition to the 10,000 the city already plants. That's where TreesCharlotte comes in. Started in 2012, this public-private initiative led by Dave Cable, whose background is with the Catawba Lands Conservancy, is tasked with organizing nonprofits, government, and local communities to plant trees on private property and reach the 2050 goal. In its first year, the group planted 4,056 trees. It hosts several events each year, planting trees through the NeighborWoods project in areas that have none and encouraging people to respect and protect the trees they have. Cable tells people who plant a tree to name it or dedicate it to someone they love. "We ask folks to name trees for family members hoping that they won't let Uncle Joe die in the backyard," he says.

Turns out, we love living near trees for good reason. The natural environment provides major health and wellness perks. The Japanese have studied Shinrin-yoku, or "forest bathing," for decades and have found scientific evidence that short trips to the woods, including a couple of walks every day, increase the cells capable of warding off infection and thwarting cancer growth by half. In one study, a group was asked to walk through a forest for a few hours while another walked the city. The scientists found that being in the woods led to a lower pulse and lower blood pressure. Now, there's an entire research field called "forest medicine," based on studies that have shown that breathing in phytoncides, or essential oils from the wood of trees, helps people relax.

Shaded, tree-lined streets are also more walkable, which encourages a more active lifestyle, decreasing obesity. Other studies prove that people recovering from injury or illness heal faster when they have views of trees.

Another Japanese study found that living near trees dramatically reduces the likelihood of developing asthma—dropping 25 percent in small children for every extra few hundred trees in an area. According to an American Forests study, Mecklenburg County's trees remove thousands of tons of carbon dioxide, seriously reducing air pollution. And they remove millions of pounds of other air pollutants, including ozone, each year. And a 2009 study in the *Journal of Epidemiology and Community Health* found a correlation between green space and increasing levels of physical and mental well-being. The relation was strongest for reducing anxiety and depression. And still other studies from the Netherlands to New York show that living near parks does much more than add beauty to a neighborhood.

We're happier around trees.

A small tree grows just across the lake from the bandstand in Freedom Park. No more than fifteen feet tall, the tree has slender branches that look bony and unimpressive compared with the park's iconic oaks and cherries. On appearances alone, it's an ordinary tree. But it has an incredible story.

During the American Revolution, when Sam Adams and other patriots planned to revolt, they met at a tree. The inspiring elm in Boston Common symbolized freedom, the patriots believed, so they later named it the Liberty Tree. Word got around, and soon, meetings in other states took place at other liberty trees. From Georgia to Massachusetts, whenever a redcoat spotted one, he chopped it down.

In 1999, the last original liberty tree, a tulip poplar on the St. John's College campus in Annapolis, Maryland, fell, a victim of Hurricane Floyd. American Forests collected more than a thousand seeds from that tree, thought to be around four hundred years old, and planted fourteen of its seedlings. Charlotte lawyer and tree activist Rick Roti learned that each of the original thirteen colonies was guaranteed a seedling from the last remaining liberty tree. Roti fought to get North Carolina's tree in Charlotte, and in 2007, our state's liberty tree was planted in Freedom Park.

Three years later, someone tried to chop it down. No one knows who did it or why someone would want to. But today, the hacked tulip poplar is bandaged by steel, with "wound wood" forming around its scar, about halfway up its trunk. Arborists argued at the time whether the tree would make it — some thought it should come down — but others fought to give it a chance. Charlotte's liberty tree is a little stressed out, but it's still standing.

A few years ago, while out on his daily run, Mike Orell noticed a green-and-white, diamond-shaped symbol attached to the trunk of a tree. *Treasure Tree,* it read. When he got home, he looked into it and found that in the early 2000s, former city arborist Tom Martin started a committee to identify Charlotte's exceptional trees — interesting species, trees that represent the largest of their kind. Martin and his committee identified 123.

Orell was inspired. He planned to find all 123. He was so passionate about it, one of his friends suggested he start a blog. Armed with the National Wildlife Federation's *Field Guide to Trees of North America,* he started writing "Charlotte Trees" (charlottetrees.blogspot.com). The goal: to educate Charlotteans about their impressive canopy and share his search for Treasure Trees. It was something he could get excited about. Since Martin's program dissolved, Orell says, "I didn't really feel like there was anyone out there championing the trees."

But of course, someone was. Patrick George, owner of Heartwood, was working on a website of his own. Entrusted with Martin's original notes, Patrick started "The Queen's Crown," a website dedicated to telling the stories behind some of the city's most interesting trees (thequeenscrown. org). The liberty tree is one of them. "The Parthenon, the cathedrals, these are all inspired by the trees," Patrick says. "This is what my life is about, the stories."

The Vitex agnus-castus at Wing Haven Gardens & Bird Sanctuary in Myers Park shares another story. With its inverted-octopus branches and soft spears of lavender-colored blooms, it is so impressive that American Forests declared it the best living example — the national champion — of the species. In 2000, it was listed on the National Register of Big Trees. The Vitex, Mecklenburg County's first national champion, joins thirty other trees from the state.

Orell can point out almost every notable tree in the city's oldest neighborhoods — a massive 125-foot poplar at the Duke Mansion, one of the only big-leaf magnolias in the city, and a water oak off Randolph Road with the most impressive root system of maybe any tree in town. But he has a favorite.

On a modest lot on Lombardy Circle there's a gnarled old deodar cedar commanding attention and easily dwarfing the small cottage it shades. "I love this tree so much," he says.

Trees like this, Orell says, helped revive his relationship with his home-town. He grew up in Dilworth, where his parents still live, and left the city after high school to study at Emory University. He stayed in Atlanta for seventeen years. When his wife got a job opportunity in Charlotte that they couldn't pass up in 2008, Orell reluctantly obliged. "Atlanta just has so much going on," he says. "I did not want to move back to Charlotte."

Orell has been back in Charlotte for six years. He has two little boys and, for now, he considers himself fortunate to be able to watch them grow up around the city's impressive trees, the same way he did. If the boys are as lucky as their dad, they'll spend many more years in a Charlotte lush with stunning oaks mixed with colorful crepe myrtles and dogwoods. They'll climb the low, sturdy branches of southern magnolias and hide from each other behind their massive trunks. And they'll search. They'll search for who they are. They'll search for inspiration. And they might find it in their backyard, wedged in a retired Michelin, swinging from the selfless branches of an old willow oak.

VIRGINIA BROWN was born in suburban Chicago but calls Charlotte home. She grew up surrounded by Charlotte's beautiful trees, so writing about them was very personal. A graduate of the University of North Carolina at Chapel Hill and the Medill School of Journalism at Northwestern University, she is a writer based in Charlotte.

Views in Fiction

Dear, Deer Abby

TAMAR MYERS

ABBY PLANTAGENET was the loneliest woman on the planet. "I, Abby Plantagenet, am the loneliest woman on the planet," she would say to strangers at Trader Joe's. People usually reacted with a bit of caution, giving Abby more elbow room at the deli, for instance. These responses served to make Abby even lonelier, although on the plus side, she didn't catch a cold virus for seven years in a row.

Abby hadn't always felt so isolated. Twenty years earlier she and her husband, Harlan, had retired to Charlotte to be near their only daughter, Jasmine, and *her* husband, both physicians at Presbyterian hospital. Then just a year later their precious daughter, Ashley, was born. For three golden years Abby virtually raised Ashley, while her parents devoted their lives to their careers and their patients. Then a "too good to pass up" research opportunity in Chicago came along for both of the young doctors. Just like that, without properly considering Abby's feelings, they packed up their household and off they went, taking *Abby's* granddaughter with them. Then something happened and Abby never saw them again.

Abby was heartbroken. She'd come of age watching *Phil Donahue,* raised her daughter, Jasmine, watching *Oprah,* so now she tried working through her grief watching *Dr. Phil,* but to no avail. She quit Saint Matthew Catholic Church in Ballantyne in order to attend Calvary, the mega-church shaped like a crown, which was closer to her house in the South Charlotte neighborhood of Five Knolls. But despite the fact that both boasted more members than the population of South Dakota, somehow Abby Plantagenet never managed to make a friend.

Abby and Harlan Plantagenet had been married fifty years, but recently her husband had taken on a full-time, live-in mistress, ESPN, or Esopina, as Abby called her. Abby liked to give names to everything; it gave her something to do. She'd even named Harlan's angina: Aunt Gina. The couple slept in separate bedrooms, but every morning Abby would greet Harlan with forced cheer and say something nice, such as, "So dear, did your Aunt Gina come to visit you during the night?" On the surface one might view such a greeting as insensitive or even rude, but truth was — and every woman knew this in her bones — a man didn't start to really listen until a woman had spoken her fifth word, so Harlan never heard a word she said. The first five words she spoke were always wasted, and before the sixth word was ever uttered, his attention was fully engaged by little Miss Esopina.

In Abby's fertile imagination Miss Esopina was of Latin heritage, with lustrous dark hair and *come hither* eyes. She certainly wasn't tubby, with thinning gray hair and age spots on her hands as concentrated as leopard print. So Abby felt lonely. Never once did she think of getting a divorce, although she did once get a cat from Mecklenburg County SPCA. The orange tabby had been born in a McDonald's dumpster and, despite being a cat, was as hungry for companionship as was Abby. Nonetheless, within two weeks Abby's incessant chatter drove the cat away.

Then one evening at dusk a doe and her fawn slipped soundlessly into the backyard. Abby watched transfixed as they nibbled at some shrubbery. The stupid old bushes mattered naught, for the deer were the first company to come unbidden to the Plantagenet home in many years. The next morning Abby, with renewed energy, drove up to the Colony Square Harris Teeter and bought a prepackaged bag of mixed salad greens to feed her visitors. Alas, her eagerness to show her hospitality was her downfall. Abby had always served her husband dinner in front of the idiot box, despite his affair with Miss Esopina. Unfortunately that afternoon he'd helped her with the groceries and couldn't help but notice the fresh salad ingredients.

"This is new," Harlan said. "Isn't it cheaper to buy a whole head of iceberg and cut it up."

"Perhaps," said Abby. "But you know what your daughter the doctor always says."

"What's that?"

True to form, Harlan had stopped listening and was back gazing at his mistress. Well, his daughter the doctor did say that iceberg lettuce was not as nutritious as the more sophisticated salad ingredients with darker leaves, such as spinach, and radicchio, and romaine. She hoped the deer had sophisticated palettes as well.

That evening Abby served Harlan a small mixed green salad, which he ate without comment as he gazed upon Miss Esopina. The remainder of the bag she put out for the deer and her fawn. Since it was December and forage was becoming scarce in what little patches of woodland remained, the animals readily accepted her gift. In fact, Abby barely had time to make it back to the house and turn around before the salad was gone. That started her thinking about corn—feed corn, the kind given to cows in the winter.

The next day, Abby let her fingers do the walking through the Yellow Pages and located a feed store. There she purchased a bushel of corn tied up in burlap sack, and that very evening measured out two cups of kernels, putting them on a concrete garden bench near the birdbath. Almost immediately, five deer appeared: two does, two fawns, and one buck. Abby was thrilled from the tips of her stubby toes to the topmost strand of her thinning gray hair. Suddenly, she no longer felt lonely.

As was her custom, Abby dined alone in the kitchen with David Muir from *ABC World News.* Even though he was a sight better looking than little Miss Esopina, Abby was not addicted to watching him. Why, some evenings she preferred to listen to NPR on FM 90.7. At any rate, after supper one evening, having dined alone in the kitchen, Abby tried to slip outside with a paper bag filled with corn, but was shocked to find that the sliding glass door was blocked by Harlan.

"What in the blazes," she said. "Harlan, you nearly gave me a heart attack."

"Abby, we need to talk," Harlan said.

"But we can't," Abby said. "I mean, you never talk, except to Miss Esopina."

"Who is Miss Esopina?" Harlan said.

"Harrumph," Abby said, for she was fond of that word. Apparently Harlan had begun to listen. "It is the name I've given to your precious ESPN."

Harlan took one of Abby's soft spotted hands in both of his equally mottled man hands. He led her gently to their nearly unused sofa that sat at a right angle to his much-used La-Z-Boy recliner.

"My dear Abby," he said. "You can't be feeding the deer."

"Why not?" she said. "They're my only friends."

"Because the deer are a menace," Harlan said.

"A *menace?*" Abby couldn't believe her ears.

"Abby, don't you ever read the local section in the *Observer?* Just last week in Matthews a woman was killed when a herd of deer tried to dash across the road right in front of her car. It happened in the *middle* of the afternoon, Abby."

"But what about the deer, Harlan?"

Harlan put his arm around Abby's shoulders. It felt like a foreign object: perhaps a long warm tube of meatloaf in a sleeve. Had it been years since she'd felt the weight of his arm?

"My dear, deer Abby," he said. "Unfortunately we have taken over the deer's habitat. We have cut down their woods in order to build more subdivisions, and they have nowhere to go. And in some cases, they won't go."

"What do you mean, Harlan?"

"You know that young couple who live down the street that jog by every day after work, even when it's raining? His name is Jared. They jog on the greenway on weekends, and he told me that he's seen far more deer in our neighborhood than he ever has in the woods along the greenway."

Abby couldn't believe her ears. Harlan was finally paying attention to her.

"Why are there more deer here than in the greenway?" she asked.

Harlan squeezed her shoulder. "Because someone has been feeding them."

She started to pull away, but his grip tightened. "Oh, I don't mean you, dear — no pun intended," he said. "There's a lady on Bellgate Drive who has as many as twenty-three deer coming to eat at her back door every night. As long as she keeps feeding them, they have no incentive to move on, to find their way to the greenway or beyond."

"Then why doesn't someone tell her to stop feeding them?" Abby said. "Just like you told me."

"If only it were that simple," Harlan said. "Before the deer got the hint and moved on, some of them would undoubtedly starve — that's nature's way, you see. The weak die, the strong survive."

"I would hate to watch anything starve," Abby said. In past years, when she had the energy to tend her flower beds, she even apologized to weeds as she pulled them out.

"True," said Harlan, "but think about her immediate neighbors. All those deer create a traffic nightmare, and none of her neighbors can keep gardens. One of the original families, who'd lived across the street for generations, long before it became a subdivision, was so heartbroken about what the deer did to their place that they ended up selling."

"That's awful," Abby said. However, inside she didn't feel awful; she felt a strange itch begin in her gut, like her insides were trying to remember something. What was she feeling? Was it lust? Could it be love?

"So then," Harlan said, "you do understand why you can't feed the deer?"

"Where have all the years gone, Harlan?" she said.

"I'll need a 'yes' answer, Abby."

"Yes," Abby said. Yes, she understood about not feeding the stupid deer. What she didn't understand was how Harlan had found the time to hear all neighborhood gossip, yet up until now, hadn't had a minute to talk to her. Maybe he visited with the neighbors when he took out the garbage, or it could be when he brought in the newspaper. As far she knew he was perpetually glued to his La-Z-Boy recliner carrying on his sordid affair with that strumpet, little Miss Esopina.

"Good," Harlan said, and he removed his meatloaf of an arm from around her shoulders and walked stiffly back to his recliner.

Just like that, their tête-à-tête was over. That was it. Abby felt unteth-ered. She wondered if an astronaut might feel the same thing if the line connecting her safely to her space module suddenly become undone. How-ever, now the only person in the world who could help her was her daughter in Chicago, but Harlan had strictly forbidden her from making any long-distance calls until he'd had had the time to show her how to circumvent the exorbitant surcharges. Of course Harlan never managed to find the time.

But now she *needed* to call Jasmine — she *had* to call Jasmine — and then the phone rang! What would one call that? Divine Providence? Luck? Abby had once heard someone on *Oprah* say that there was no such thing as coincidence. Abby no longer believed in the ooey-gooey death part of religion, but she was fine with believing in blessings and omens, just as long as they were meant for her, and not her enemies.

Abby's most familiar inner voice told her to go ahead and pick up the phone. Undoubtedly the caller was Jasmine. The most likely scenario was that her daughter could feel the turmoil in her mother's heart over the hundreds of miles, and that she was reaching out to her. On the other hand, maybe Abby's desires were writing their own script.

"Hello?" Abby whispered into the phone.

The voice on the other end was both startling and familiar. "Who is this please?"

Abby was paralyzed with indecision. What should she do? Should she hang up? Should she ask for her daughter, Jasmine? Or should she identify herself to Ashley, as the other grandma, the *strange* one? "She's a little bit *off*," a parishioner once said about her, as Abby tarried in the privacy of her stall in the ladies' room. At first Abby was deeply hurt by this remark, which is usually applied to milk, but then she decided to draw comfort from the fact that at least she wasn't *cuckoo-cuckeroo* like her mother had been.

"If you don't tell me who you are, I'm going to hang up," the voice said.

Abby sighed. "I'm your Grandma Plantagenet," she said. "I'm your mama's mama."

"Oh, *that* one. Hi, Grandma."

Abby was thrilled. "Hi, Ashley. What are you doing?"

"I'm looking for Jesus," the voice on the other end of the line said.

"What do you *mean* you're 'looking for Jesus'?" Heaven forfend, the child was becoming a religious fanatic; that was far worse than being a whack-a-doodle in Abby's book.

"I'm in a Christmas play, Grandma, and I took baby Jesus home for the weekend, and now I can't find him."

Abby was immeasurably relieved by the information. "Where did you last see him?" she said.

Ashley giggled, as she had every right to do. "Grandma! If I knew, then I wouldn't be looking for him, would I?"

Touché, Abby thought. "What role do you have in this play, dear?"

"I play the Vegan Mary, Grandma."

"The word is *virgin*, dear," Abby said helpfully. "*Not* vegan."

"No, Grandma, this play is definitely about the Vegan Mary. My character doesn't eat any meat, dairy, or eggs, and she and the Three Wise Guys get mixed up in this — hey, do you want to come over and see us perform? I can get you into the play for free since you're family."

Family. That was one of the most beautiful words in the English language. The first syllable starts strong, with the teeth positioned on the bottom lip, as if to bite, but the word ends in a smile. Yes, a thousand times *yes,* Abby would love to hop on a plane and fly to Chicago in order to watch this flesh of her flesh play the part of the Vegan Mary. However, in order to do that, she would have to enlist Harlan's help. Negotiating Charlotte Douglas International Airport, especially the parking situation, was more than someone who was *a little off* could handle on her own.

"Just a minute, dear," Abby said into the phone, as she carried it into the living room. "Now Harlan, I am so glad that you are sitting down, because do I ever have a surprise for you."

Abby was flabbergasted when the first thing Harlan did was tell little Miss Esopina to shut up — which she did, too. Harlan pointed his thing at her, and her eyes went totally blank. Then he got up and walked over to Abby and took the phone from her hand.

"I don't care how many credits you only have left to graduate," he said into the phone. "We donate a substantial amount to the university every year, so I have a good deal of pull with the board. If this kind of thing happens one more time, I'll have your skinny white asses thrown out of school faster than you can say Benjamin Franklin."

"Listen, sir," the female voice said, having suddenly aged a decade, "it's just part of a sorority prank —"

"No, you listen," Harlan said. "Twenty years ago my daughter and husband, and their infant daughter — my granddaughter — were killed in a car wreck when a buck jumped through the windshield and pinned my son-in-law to the front seat of their car. They were only three blocks from our house, having just started out driving to Chicago. My wife was doing really well until recently—well never you mind; it's none of your damn business. Do you hear me? Do you *hear* me?"

TAMAR MYERS is the author of forty-three novels and a book of short stories for children. In addition she has published many short stories for adults, as well as over a hundred articles on gardening. She lives in Charlotte with her husband, two cats, and a dog. On a walk one morning, she and her dog came face to face with a herd of eleven deer trotting straight at them down the middle of their suburban street.

Vladimir and Michael

AILEN ARREAZA

NO AMOUNT OF COERCING from Vladimir could convince his little
brother to touch the giant contraptions filled with candy and soft drinks
in the motel's breezeway. Michael was four, but he wasn't stupid. What if
the clerk sitting behind the desk in the front lobby saw him? What if he
came over and tried to talk to him *in English*? No, Michael was going to
play it safe. If Vladimir wanted to find out what the buttons next to the
glass panes on those big machines did, he would have to step up and push
them himself.

Vladimir had never seen anything like them before. Not even back at
the Habana Libre, the big hotel on Twenty-Third Street in Havana he used
to sneak into with his mom so that she could fill her purse with toilet paper
from the bathrooms. When he visited his cousin's house, Vladimir would
see newspaper in the wastebasket next to the toilet, but his mom always
managed to have real toilet paper at home and in her purse. She traded
rice or milk for it with neighbors, and when she couldn't find anyone to
barter with she'd sneak into the bathrooms of one of the city's most
luxurious hotels and take it.

Vladimir loved the Habana Libre — the shiny floors and air conditioning, the big chandelier hanging over the reception desk, the fresh, clean scent he couldn't find anywhere else in the city. But his favorite thing about the hotel was the automatic sliding glass door in the entrance. Vladimir liked to wait for the rare break in the hustle and bustle of tourists entering and exiting when the door would close and it was his feet — just his feet — on the mat that would cause it to magically open again.

The motel with the big candy machines also had an automatic sliding door and Vladimir and Michael had spent the morning stepping on and off the mat, watching the door open and close. They didn't have to wait very long for the door panels to come together; there weren't many tourists visiting a motel on the east side of Charlotte, North Carolina, in the middle of December. Vladimir still didn't understand how the door's mechanism worked, but, somehow, his new, unlimited access to it made it seem less magical, and after a while, he let Michael's feet be solely responsible for causing it to open.

A week earlier, at his parents' friends' apartment back in Havana's Vedado neighborhood, Michael played on the floor with a toy car their father had made him out of scrap wood at work, while Vladimir stared at a giant map of the United States hanging on the wall.

When they got the news that they'd been approved to leave Cuba as political refugees, Vladimir's parents decided to move the family in with friends. Vladimir couldn't even go back to school to say goodbye to Ms. Blanco, his fourth grade teacher who had whispered in his ear at last year's end-of-term ceremony that he had the best academic record in his class but would not be recognized because of his mother's anti-revolutionary political views. His mom had been arrested a few times for participating in peaceful antigovernment demonstrations and, to avoid any last-minute surprises from the police, they had decided to hide out with friends until their departure date arrived.

"They told me at the U.S. Interest Section that we would be resettled to this place," his mom said, holding out a piece of paper that said, Charlotte,

North Carolina. "I think it might be cold there, maybe we'll even see snow!"

Vladimir could draw, freehand, an entire map of Cuba, each province delineated and labeled, including its capitals. But as he stared at the United States, he didn't know where to begin to look for Charlotte. He decided to start on the top left corner and work his way across, as if he were reading a book.

It took him well into an hour, but he finally found Charlotte on the map. A dot, slightly bigger than the ones surrounding it. "That must mean it's a bigger city," he thought.

Things in Charlotte were bigger — the roads, the cars, the houses, the bananas, the tubes of toothpaste. Everything seemed to have been put on steroids. Yet, the city, on the whole, felt much more tame than Havana, less busy, less chaotic, more manageable. Vladimir thought about how strange it was that so many big, bold pieces made up such a controlled whole.

He had not seen much of the city yet; only the route from the motel to the refugee office where they provided the whole family with winter coats and were helping them rent an apartment. Vladimir really liked the girl who worked in the refugee office — she spoke Spanish with a funny accent and had big bowls of candy on her desk.

"What kind of names are Vladimir and Michael for a couple of Cuban kids anyway?" she'd asked them.

Vladimir smiled. "They're political statements," he said. "When I was born, mom was still a Communist, so she gave me a Russian name in honor of Cuba's biggest ally. But, by the time my brother was born, she'd realized that the revolution was built on a bunch of lies so she decided to give him a really American name. That's why his name is Michael, not Miguel."

Vladimir had told that same line, about the revolution being built on a bunch of lies, to a police officer in Cuba, when he saw him arrest his mom for talking to a foreign journalist about the scarcity and oppression she had to deal with every day.

There was no scarcity in Charlotte, however, and when the nice girl from the refugee office took the family to a grocery store for the first time to buy bread, milk, and other staples, both of Vladimir's parents felt dizzy and sick to their stomachs.

Now Vladimir stood staring at the candy machine at the motel. He just had to know what those buttons did. He stepped up and pushed one with the letter *B* on it. Nothing. Then he pushed another, with the number 7. Nothing still. He pushed a few more and felt Michael pull the back of his shirt. He turned around and saw the motel clerk walking toward them. Vladimir froze. The clerk said something to them in English and smiled. Then, he pulled a green bill out of his pocket and put it in the machine. He pushed a few buttons and a yellow bag with the letters M&M'S fell to the bottom. He pulled the bag out and handed it to the kids. *Gracias*, they both said in unison.

As the months and years went by, Vladimir would discover Charlotte's best places for barbecue and fried chicken. He would learn to make biscuits from scratch and order iced tea with every meal. He'd develop a taste for the sushi and Indian stews and Mexican tacos brought to Charlotte by immigrants from all over the world. But during those first few weeks, America . . . Charlotte . . . home . . . tasted like candy-coated, chocolate-covered peanuts.

AILEN ARREAZA was born in Havana, Cuba, and has lived in Charlotte since 1996. She is a regular contributor to *Creative Loafing Charlotte*'s News & Culture section. She is married to Tony and has two young boys, Luki and Pau. In her attempt to become a responsible adult human, she has finally figured out which knob controls which burner on the stove and no longer believes that continually buying new underwear is the best way to deal with laundry.

Loraylee

An excerpt from Tomorrow's Bread

ANNA JEAN MAYHEW

I WAKE IN THE late spring night, the train crossing Second Street singing to me—*whoo-whoo*. I want to grab Hawk, jump on. Ride out of Charlotte. The *clack-clack* of the train speed up 'til the throbbing of the engine fill my head, my bed, the room. The whistle hoot again at the West Boulevard junction. The four-thirty, heading south. If I'm gone go, I'd go north. Chicago. Find my mama.

Down in the gully, Little Sugar make whispery music, sliding through the dark like a ghost, calling my boy to it. Unless I catch him, he run across the yard, a bucket in one hand, a net made from an old stocking in the other, bent on frogs or fish or whatever lure him down to where that creek live. He don't know how quick the water can pull him under, him all safe in bed, sleeping sound.

In the dull light coming out Bibi room, I see the chain from the attic door in the hallway, swinging. She always touch it when she pass by. Why she up this time of night?

I gone get a clock that plug in, one that glow in the dark. Won't have to remember to wind it, won't have to wait for Uncle Ray chickens to start clucking in they coop to tell me daylight coming on. I got to rouse Hawk soon, get him fed and dressed. When he born, Bibi say, "Enjoy him being a baby 'cause it won't last." She right, and now he six, long legs, big feet. He in first grade with a teacher name Mrs. Hirschold—a white woman, must be sixty—come to Myers Street School all the way from Dilworth. Why she teaching in such a wore-out place, chain-link fence around the dirt playground, hand-me-down books? Seven years since that Brown Board thing and nothing change.

When Hawk start school last September, I took him there ever day for a week to be sure he know the way. I tell him about traffic lights, to look up and down the street before he cross. We leave the house and he grab my hand, his hand skinny in mine, tugging on me to stop so he can holler, "Hey!" to Mr. Stern, sweeping the sidewalk in front of the grocery, and to Jonny No Age at the flower shop. Waving to everbody he know, covering up being scared.

At the corner of South Myers, he tilt his head back and stare at the big school building, chimneys on top. He point to the metal stairs going up, then level, then back to the scraggly yard. "Why the stairs outside, Mama?"

"Jacob's Ladder, what the kids call it, get them out if a fire starts."

His gray eyes are round, big. "Ever been a fire?"

"I reckon not. School still there." We go on inside, down those rackety halls to the room what already different from the others because Mrs. Hirschold keep bringing in something new. Hanging things on the walls, setting the desks in rows one day, a circle the next. Hawk say Mrs. Hirschold smell good, and she do, like flowers. Another thing, she look straight at me through her smudged glasses, calling me Mrs. Hawkins, thinking a mother must be married.

She squatty, Bibi would say. Short and wide. Her baggy dress hang way past her knees. Black lace-ups with thick stockings sagging at her ankles.

Later on I tell Uncle Ray, "She got a grandmother look."

He smile. "That's good."

The day I drop in to take Hawk lunch he forgot, I open the door to his room. See him leaning against Mrs. Hirschold, her fat pale hand patting his back. I like her just fine after that.

Now he walk himself over to Third Street, along with half a dozen other kids heading from Brooklyn to Myers Street School. I stand on the porch and watch him going away from me. Skinny, like his daddy, his round head bobbing while he talk to himself the way he do, then around the corner and out of sight. On they way to school, the kids pass the church, the barbershop, the club with music on Saturday nights. On McDowell they go by the House of Prayer and the Savoy. After he learn to read, he always tell me what playing there. Nine blocks to school, nine blocks home, a long way for short legs. We been asking for a school bus. Uncle Ray say we might as well ask for a limousine.

I'm standing with a bunch of people under an awning at Trade and College, heading home after three, trying to stay out of the rain. Most days I walk the ten blocks to and from work, saving the bus fare. Unless it a drencher like today. Or too hot, too cold. I got a paper bag tucked under my arm for when I get off at Elizabeth and Morrow.

A man in the crowd say, "No justice in that," in a loud white voice. He want people to hear him, making me glad I don't know what he mean so I won't get riled. I board behind him, drop my dime in the box, nod to the driver, Gus, one of the nice ones, been driving a bus all his life. He got some comment whenever he see me. "Any news about Brooklyn?" he say, his blue eyes smiling behind his glasses.

"They's talk it going down." I hate saying that, hate hearing others say it.

The noisy white man is on the bench seat behind Gus, and I walk on by. I like the back of the bus, even if I am allowed to ride up front now, where I'd have to sit next to those stiff-necked men in they hats and suits who don't want me there anyway.

I get off at my stop, hold the bag over my head, running. Morrow Street is a muddy mess. Got muck on my shoes, my legs, my uniform before I get home, glad to be there, ducking around the magnolia in the front yard. Its branches near about cover our front yard. Uncle Ray respect that tree, like he say when he trim it, "Only one magnolia in all of Second Ward, and that's it." I run up the sagging porch steps, drip onto the mat, the bag coming apart in my hands. I toss it on the rocker, open the door. "Hey, y'all," I call out. Nobody home, not even Bibi. No telling where she is. I reckon Uncle Ray has taken our one umbrella and gone to meet Hawk. Just the sort of thing he do. I'm glad to be in the house alone so I can shuck my uniform to the kitchen floor. Even my slip is soaked, my cold nipples showing through.

I get water going in the pot for a cup of hot coffee and head for the room I share with Hawk. There is Bibi, in his bed, under the plaid spread, snoring. If she sleep all day, she be up all night, a problem for me or Uncle Ray. I leave her be, grab some dry clothes, empty out the hamper to run a load before I start supper. Bibi not gone do it laying in bed. I toss everything in the washer on the back porch, propping open the kitchen door. I like smelling soap powder instead of the sour air the house has after a rain. Mildew, ashes in the woodstove, the coal bucket by the back door.

At the sink, stringing beans, I'm glad I have a clean uniform in the closet for tomorrow; no way that load of wash gone get dry in this damp house overnight. All us who work at the S&W wear uniforms, except Mr. Griffith. Retta Lawrence, who work next to me on the line, say uniforms save wear and tear on her wardrobe. They sure save time. Grab me a clean one, off I go. Last lady Bibi worked for docked her pay three dollars if Bibi needed a new uniform, but the lady kept them when she fired her.

If she think of it, Bibi say something about that like it was yesterday, not three-four years ago. "Miz Easterling, she misplace something and she fire me, saying, 'Girl, you stealing.' Then she kep those uniforms I paid for, like she gone get another maid same size."

Bibi more likely the one misplacing stuff, the way she do at home. She couldn't get another job, no reference from Miz Easterling. After while, I come to like having her home to cook and clean, be with Hawk. Back then. Before she got so bad off I was afraid of what she might forget next. Before Uncle Ray moved in to take care his sister.

After supper Uncle Ray and I sit on the porch. He scratch the top of his head where his scalp shows through, shiny walnut under a light snow. The air is clean, cool, when the rain stop. Even the muddy street look like it been washed. Little Sugar move along in the gully, brown and sluggish except in the spring when it deep and clear. The breeze bring a whiff of sewer. No sugar in that creek. Our magnolia catch the setting sun that sparkle in the leaves, bleach the flowers. Uncle Ray say, "Now would you look at that? Remind me of when I saw the light." I listen careful. Something different ever time he tell that story, rambling up to the start. "Mostly we can't tell when a good thing gone come of a bad thing." He crack his knuckles, settle himself. "I left this world after I took a bad fall, and while I was gone I saw a light." He tilt on the back legs of the straight chair he favor; cough to clear his throat the way he do. Bibi push food at him ever chance she get, trying to put some fat on his skinny body. His seventy-four years show in the wrinkles around his face, the wattle under his chin like a rooster. He a fit old man, can still chop wood and clear the yard after a storm, if his lumbago don't act up. He take his pipe from his shirt pocket, tamp it with his forefinger, light it. "Dr. Wilkins brought me back and the light faded. From then on I know the truth." Flick the match into the yard just to see how far it fly before it land in the wet grass. "I were dead, don't you doubt it, just St. Peter weren't calling me yet." Puff, puff, smoke rising. "The light is what a baby see when it squeal out from its mama." He look hard at me. "Souls grow again in a new baby." He give his leg three pats, once for each word. "Death. Is. Birth." He get up, go down the steps toward the street, stopping to pick up the match.

"*Mm-mm,*" I say. "Maybe you right. Make as much sense to me as what I hear in church."

Uncle Ray see me looking off past him to Morrow Street like someone might come along to tell us why things happen the way they do. He look at the letter I pull from my pocket. Had it for a couple days. Been thinking on it.

"What you got there?" His skinny legs fold into a squat beside the walk, him poking at the ground, smoke rising from the pipe.

"Notice from the city."

"What it say?"

"A man gone come see about our house."

"*Hmm,*" he say. "Dooby Franklin right once in a while." He stand, stretch, his rough hands behind his hips. I can tell the lumbago hurting him by the way he move slow up the front walk onto the porch, sit on the steps with a grunt.

"You back bothering you?"

"*Um-hmm.*" He put his bony hand on my foot, pat it. "Set that letter aside. We can't know how a thing gone turn out." He talk like that ever since he seen the light.

I fold the paper over and over 'til it not much bigger than a matchbook.

ANNA JEAN (A.J.) MAYHEW, a native Charlottean, set her first novel, *The Dry Grass of August,* in the Myers Park neighborhood where she grew up. It won the Sir Walter Raleigh Award for Fiction. Her novel-in-progress, *Tomorrow's Bread,* excerpted above, is also set in Charlotte and tells of the historically black neighborhood of Brooklyn—demolished by urban renewal in the 1960s. The title is from Langston Hughes's "Democracy," which seeks swift racial equality: "I cannot live on tomorrow's bread."

195

A Place Called Home

One Road, Many Names

IRANIA MACÍAS PATTERSON

♪ *Raindrops keep falling on my head*
And just like the guy whose feet are too big for his bed . . . ♪

AS A YOUNG GIRL, I always dreamt of being Katharine Ross and
sharing the love of Paul Newman and Robert Redford as I watched the
movie *Butch Cassidy and the Sundance Kid.* For these two men, I would
have certainly agreed to break the law, teach Spanish for free, and travel
throughout the world robbing banks. *"Manos arriba"*—Hands up . . .
"Todos contra la pared"—All of you against the wall.

My impression of the United States was based on American Western
films. I had no idea that I was destined, years later, to live not in the West
but in the South of the U.S., not robbing banks with Robert Redford and
Paul Newman, but living in the nation's second largest financial center:
Charlotte, N.C.

When my mother, Juanita, decided to send me to Charlotte, she thought
it would be a temporary stay—only a few months until I learned English.
My mother thought I was coming back.

I thought so, too, but . . .

The moment I walked down the jet bridge to the plane—a tunnel that connected the two worlds of my Venezuelan past to an unknown future—and sank into my assigned seat, I felt in the pit of my stomach that I would not be coming back.

As I looked down on the fading aquamarine coastline where Venezuela met the Caribbean Sea, I knew I too was flying from the nest. Farewell to the Caracas of eternal spring, a lush valley ringed by the Avila Mountain and only a whisper away from the beach. Above the clouds, I sensed the imminent birth of a story filled with adventure; there was nothing to lose.

Cloaked only in one thin jacket and slapped by the frigid wind of early January 1993, I waited outside the Charlotte Douglas International Airport for a ride.

That day began the first winter of my life. My Aunt Tairis drove me back to her house. We passed by many gray, uniform buildings, along rolling streets with shallow hills framed in naked trees, without the numerous bridges or tunnels that were familiar sights in Caracas, and without many pedestrians in the street. It reminded me of the *Sleeping Beauty* story: all enchanted and asleep.

I did not speak English, but could read it. So, I sounded out every sign, aloud. Like a grown kindergartener, I read (and mispronounced) the name of each street, restaurant, and shop that crossed my vision.

In my early explorations, before the GPS era, I longed for a compass to guide my steps to my destinations. And I dreamt of a GPS to guide me in translating this new world, in tracking my identity and soul in space as they traveled to and through a new culture. I feared getting lost in every sense. Lost when speaking a new language, lost in who I was and who I wanted to be, lost in what is and what was. Lost in what to trade and what to treasure.

Literally, I could not find my way anywhere. I remember cruising down Kings Drive, wondering when it would turn into Queens Road, and landing in the blink of an eye at Providence Road. Sometimes Park Road was here . . . and there. And Sharon—who was that woman married to?

To an Amity, and sometimes to a View? And why did she stretch all the way across town, altering her name?

I drove along a single street with the names Tyvola, Fairview, Sardis, Rama, Idlewild, without ever turning left or right . . . What an interesting thing, one long road, with many names. What an inclusive city! Maybe one day, my name would be part of one of these long roads? The same road called in many names, a pattern that follows my own experience of living in Charlotte. What would the string of names be?

I wondered about the meaning of the streets, and to be honest I felt intimidated about the religious reverberations of these names . . . I could certainly not keep up with that sense of holiness, living in the Bible Belt, as people warned me. Trouble awaited me, for sure.

> Providence: The protective care of God or of nature as a spiritual power.
>
> Sardis: It was addressed in Revelations in terms that seem to imply that its population was notoriously soft and fainthearted.
>
> Sharon: From the Bible in Isaiah 65:10. "Sharon shall become a pasture for flocks, and the Valley of Achor a place for herds to lie down, for my people who have sought me."

Later on, I learned that in pre-suburban days, churches were about the only landmarks in the countryside of Mecklenburg County. So roads tended to be named for the churches they led to. Providence Road led to Providence Presbyterian; Sugar Creek Road passed Sugar Creek Presbyterian. Around Sharon Church the two major roads were Sharon Road, which wandered south from Charlotte out to the church, and Sharon Amity, which ran from that church northwest to the next church, Amity Presbyterian, established in 1882 off Albemarle Road. Interesting—and it relieved some of the religious pressure I felt.

Being in the city of the churches, *la ciudad de las Iglesias,* one Sunday morning I ventured to visit that Pink Castle called Calvary Church.

I realized that it was too late for the service there, so without any effort, I immediately found another church.

Lost as usual, and with a sense that something was wrong with me, always struggling to find myself between the past and the present, navigating in the deep ocean but afraid to lose sight of the safe shore, I accidentally washed up on the Central Church of God on Sardis Road. Welcomed by a pleasant stranger, I went right inside just at the time of praising. I truly experienced one of the best treasures of Charlotte, the choir of Central Church of God. Like an intense arrow, the song the choir sang touched my deepest self.

> No more shame, fear, my past is over.
> I won't go back, I can´t go back to the way it used to be
> Before your presence came and changed me.

Those words were sealed in my heart. It was a confirmation telling me to close that nostalgic past and invite the present; stop the fear of not being anywhere and choose instead to write my name and legacy in the place I stood in that very moment.

I came at a time when the black and white South was fading into colors. I was unique and found it intriguing that people wanted to know who I was. But rather than asking me *who* they asked me *what* I was. Charlotte demands you give yourself a name. Polite Southerners and politically correct acquaintances alike would ask me, "What do you call yourself? Hispanic? Latina?" "Are you a white Latina or a black Latina?"

Why not just Irania? I thought.

It took me a while to articulate a respectful response. I did not want to dishonor my heritage, nor did I want to oversimplify my identity to fit into the few boxes offered. I did not want to be *other* when identifying myself, but again a name, they demanded a name, a label. So I said . . .

Before being a Latina I am a woman who at night wonders about the possibility of miracles.

Before being a Latina I am a woman who carried in her womb the journey of two children.

Before being a Latina I stand in front of the mirror amazed by the history that gave meaning to my name.

And it is in that history that I found my driven forces, the passion, the essence, the purpose of life now in America.

Driven forces rooted in my childhood watered by the words of my grandmother, *mi abuela*: "Don't close your eyes when you are afraid, open them so you can face the invisible monsters."

Driven forces rooted in my childhood watered by the words of my father, *mi padre*: "You know," he said ". . . women are thresholds for life and death."

Driven forces rooted in my childhood watered by the words of my mother, *mi madre*: "My children are first."

Driven forces rooted in a romantic language, *Español,* where "I love you" is not enough. You must say: *te amo, te quiero, te adoro, te venero, te idolatro, me matas, me muero por ti, me fascinas.*

Driven forces rooted in the voice of my ancestors, immigrants like me, *como yo.*

And here I am a woman, a Latina, a mother, a poet, an American, an immigrant who found a home in Charlotte.

Creative pronunciations with heavy musical accents, you can hear people from around the world claiming to be Charlotteans. . . . Throughout the years my ears have gathered the following phrases from all walks of Charlotte, a soundtrack of diversity with a hope of home:

Charlotte is home . . .

Because it is the spearhead of the New South . . . لأن وه رأس الحربة في جنوب جديد

Because it is a fair city . . . *Porque é uma cidade justa*

Because you can see all the four seasons . . . *Parce que vous pouvez voir tous les quatre saisons*

Because it is so green . . . *Weil es so grün is*

Because the ocean and the mountains are not that far . . . Επειδή ο ωκεανός και τα βουνά δεν είναι τόσο μακριά

Because it has the best library system in the nation . . . כי יש ל העמרכת הספרייה הטובה ביותר במדינה

Because there is a space for the corporate, the bohemian, the artist, the gays, the family, the single one, the one who is looking for a second chance . . .

Because you can change for the better . . . *Ngoba kungaba ngcono*

Because Yankees smile at you . . . *Perché Yankis ti sorride*

Because you can always fall in love again . . . *Porque siempre te puedes volver a enamorar*

I would have to say that Charlotte is home because of its people. Once surrounded by the mountains of my old Caracas, I'm now surrounded by my loyal friends. The blue of the Caribbean Sea now becomes the intense yellow, orange, and red trees during fall. The salsa, boleros, and folkloric melodies are still alive in the fun of Charlotte's night with its cosmopolite options of tango, salsa nights, and the amazing variety of music offered at the Evening Muse in NoDa. The sound of my Angel Falls, the highest waterfall in the world, is now my 5:30 a.m. meditation moment, when I hear the sublime sound of my own heartbeat.

And when it rains in Charlotte, that child who loved to watch *Butch Cassidy and the Sundance Kid* remembers her first connection to the English language by singing . . .

Raindrops keep fallin' on my head

And just like the guy whose feet are too big for his bed

Nothin' seems to fit

Those raindrops are fallin' on my head, they keep fallin' . . .

But there's one thing I know

The blues they send to meet me

Won't defeat me

It won't be long till happiness

Comes up to greet me . . .

Today raindrops keep falling on my car, where I live most of the time, taking my native-born Charlottean children to school, to football games, to choir, to the Mint Museum, to Discovery Place, to Freedom Park, *aquí y allá*, here and there. And after all these years, I still get lost, but I better get used to it because it is when I feel lost that I know something new is about to be discovered.

IRANIA MACÍAS PATTERSON, a native of Venezuela, is a performer, author, and educator. Her bilingual children's picture book *Chipi Chipis, Small Shells of the Sea/Chipi Chipi Caracolitos del Mar* won an International Reading Association Children's Choice Award for 2006. She is the author of *Wings and Dreams* and is co-author of several books for librarians. For the past fifteen years she has worked as a multicultural children specialist and consultant in the area of literature and the performing arts.

Fall Festival

GRACE C. OCASIO

We, my Edwin and I, take Chloe to a pumpkin patch
where she dives into a horde of pumpkins
as though they will draw her close
as cousins she's never met.

She commands the hayride —
first child to scramble up
into the tractor-drawn wagon,
first child to throw a bucket of hay over her head.

We walk through a meadow, snatch wildflowers,
cram our pockets with them,
lean against white oaks and watch the sun
slide down the sky like a child racing down a water coaster.

We flash our headlights from Mooresville to Charlotte,
letting people know harvest is the time to gloat
over chill in the air, the snap of grass under feet,
the scent of pumpkin buttercream,

the yellow, red, and orange leaves of tupelos
that entice us to sleep even when we've been up all night,
tossing stray sandman thoughts out the window
or in the trash can in our backyard.

Twice a finalist for the Rash Poetry Award, GRACE C. OCASIO is a recipient of the 2014 North Carolina Arts Council Regional Artist Project Grant. She received honorable mention in the 2012 James Applewhite Poetry Prize, the Sonia Sanchez and Amiri Baraka Poetry Prize in 2011, and a Napa Valley Writers' Conference scholarship. Her first full-length poetry collection, *The Speed of Our Lives*, is forthcoming from BlazeVOX Books.

How Do I Get There from Sharon Amity?

MIGNON F. BALLARD

THE SUMMER WE MOVED to the Carolinas, Sharon Amity Road became the focal point of my introduction to Charlotte.

On July 4, 1970, our family made the wearisome trip from Atlanta to Charlotte. My husband and ten-year-old Melissa, along with a cooler of cold drinks to compensate for the family Ford's lack of air conditioning, followed the moving van. I trailed behind them in our old green Pontiac with our younger daughter, Amy, seven, who was recuperating from a recent tonsillectomy. The heat index that day registered somewhere between the sands of the Sahara and that place you *really* don't want to go.

Okay, maybe I exaggerate, but believe me, it was HOT! Amy and I were grateful for the monster of an air conditioner that took up most of the space on the floor beneath the Pontiac's dashboard. That car is now in the Smithsonian.

My husband had already selected our new home in the Queen City, an apartment on Sharon Road. Because it was dark when we arrived, I didn't get a look at our surroundings until morning. I was delighted to discover we were only a few blocks from the recently built SouthPark Mall, and our girls were happy with our apartment's proximity to the neighborhood swimming pool. By the time Sunday rolled around, having explored the scrumptious new mall and made note of the post office and convenient grocery stores, we agreed that Amy was well enough to take a plunge in the pool.

Ah, to relax at last after days of tiresome unpacking! But our leisurely poolside unwinding quickly came to an end when Melissa dove off the side and hit one of her new permanent teeth on the concrete bottom.

Frantically we flipped through the Yellow Pages of our new Charlotte phone book to locate a dentist nearby. My husband studied the city map and I pored over the phone book while attempting to comfort our unhappy little swimmer. Naturally, dentists' offices were closed on Sunday, but after several phone calls, we were relieved to contact a kind doctor who agreed to meet us at his office nearby.

And where were we to find him? *Why, just off Sharon Amity, of course!*

How grateful we were when X-rays showed that not only was Melissa's tooth still sound, but the dentist declined to charge for our visit. Our family remained in his excellent care until he retired.

This same road, we were happy to learn, also led to many hours of delightful entertainment at the Charlotte Coliseum and Ovens Auditorium, both conveniently situated on East Independence, only a few miles off Sharon Amity.

Fast-forward a couple of years when I entered my short story for young readers in a contest sponsored by the Charlotte Writers' Club.

Writing is a lonely occupation and, in some ways, a puzzle unto itself. We cherish the time alone, but are desperate for the company of others who are plagued with the insane desire to produce the written word. Then as now, I concentrate best with quiet and privacy, which were not always available with a young family. Thank heavens for school days and blessed silence! I tried not to seem too eager to shove our children out the door before barricading myself with composition book, sharp #2 pencils, and my manual Smith Corona typewriter. (Yes, it has been *that long!*) *Aunt Matilda's Ghost,* my first published book and the only one I've written for young readers, as well as a number of short stories were composed in that manner, until I reluctantly progressed to an electric typewriter, and then it took me a while to become accustomed to all that annoying *humming.* Of course it was necessary to make copies as well, and that meant dealing with a messy carbon that had to be inserted along with your typing paper into the roller.

What a delightful surprise to learn from the *Charlotte Observer* that not only did the city have the Charlotte Writers' Club, but that worthy organization sponsored writing contests on a regular basis, and the deadline for entries for the current comptition was only a few weeks away. I pored diligently over the guidelines before beginning my tale about a mongrel dog (much like ours) named Sad Sam. About mid-story, however, the girls and I all came down with bronchitis, accompanied by fever and chills, but I kept on writing, determined not to miss that important deadline.

And I'm glad I did. A few weeks later I learned that my story, "Sad Sam and the Summer Shack," had won first place in the club's juvenile story contest, and I was invited to read it at the upcoming club meeting. The meeting place (if I remember correctly, it was in a cafeteria) was only a short distance off . . . you guessed it . . . Sharon Amity!

The chairman of that contest was Ruth Moose, a talented writer in her own right, who became my longtime friend. I was invited to visit — only *visit,* mind you — a session of her writers' workshop and was pleased (I suppose *grateful* would be a more appropriate word) a few weeks later when they asked me to join their group. After all those school years of being the only person in my class who actually *cheered* when we received a writing assignment, I was at last among people who not only loved the craft as I did, but were seriously intent on developing those skills.

Our workshop met in the kitchen, and later the dining room, of Dannye Romine Powell, who later became book editor of the *Charlotte Observer.*

At that time, in order to get to Dannye's home, one simply drove several miles on Sharon Amity and turned right.

After Dannye left us to work for the *Observer*, we found a meeting place in the community room of a bank near Cotswold Mall, a block or so off Sharon Amity, and when the bank eventually needed the space for other purposes, we moved several miles down Randolph Road to yet another bank. (We've been removed from some of the best!)

Meanwhile, workshop members were busily turning out poetry, short stories, essays, and novels, until one by one, we began to slowly achieve some success in the publishing world. Our friend and moderator, Margaret Caldwell, who I'm sure was a drill sergeant in another life, saw that everyone kept to their allotted time to read and critique. I believe most of us in time developed not only a keen ear, but a tough hide.

For many years, my life revolved around that distinctive place, Sharon Amity Road. It became a family joke that no matter my intended destination, I always asked, "How do I get there from Sharon Amity?" I used it to find my way to doctors' appointments, shopping at Cotswold, chatty lunches in local restaurants, and even frantic races to ERs that always seemed to happen in the middle of the night.

Although not geographically correct, Sharon Amity became my own heart of the city. It was there I earned what I consider to be the equivalent of a graduate degree in writing, with the help of cherished friends who for almost thirty years supported one another, rejoicing in each success and agonizing over every rotten rejection. (I received so many of the latter that my family borrowed the familiar expression, *This does not suit our present needs,* when I served brussels sprouts for supper!)

And if anyone should ask how I started as a writer, I'll have to tell them it all began when I turned right on Sharon Amity.

MIGNON F. BALLARD is the author of seven *Augusta Goodnight* mysteries and thirteen other novels, most recently, *Miss Dimple Picks a Peck of Trouble,* which is set during WWII and features longtime first grade teacher, Miss Dimple Kilpatrick. www.mignonballard.com.

A Place of Grandeur and Light

ELISHA T. "MOTHER" MINTER

IT WAS A COOL SEPTEMBER DAY when my husband came home and announced that he had gotten the job. My first response was, What job? It seems he had been asked by the *Charlotte Times* to apply for a job as a reporter and went about doing so in hopes of surprising me and the children with an exciting new adventure. Little did I know at the time that this home girl was going to be leaving mother and father, relatives and childhood friends, church and job, to move from our rural life outside of Fayetteville to live in what I now know to be the "Queen City" of Charlotte, North Carolina.

We celebrated this wonderful opportunity with family and friends. Packing all our earthly belongings and making preparations to move by the end of the month held many challenges. After all, we weren't rich, but we had a whole lot of love in our family and from close connections. Everybody pitched in and helped to reassure me that everything would be fine. I, however, had my doubts about fitting into this new, faster pace of living.

On moving day, my husband's new employer, Knight Publishing, sent a big truck to pick up all of our belongings. I must say, I was totally impressed with the quickness and fancy packing they brought for our humble furniture and other things. They were very gentle with my prized "whatnots" that I had procured from my mother and gifts given to us at all the many going-away celebrations.

And then it was time. One of our friends from the *Fayetteville Times* loaned us a big, baby blue station wagon with wood-paneled siding, a forerunner of today's SUV. Thirty years ago there were no such luxury vehicles to be had by the average person. The station wagon was it. We carefully packed it with suitcases for our four children—three boys and our daughter—and ourselves, with just enough clothing for the first few days when we'd stay at the old Ramada Inn that used to loom large on Kings Drive next to the McDonald's and across from rows of quaint little shops and restaurants.

This also had been the location of the famous Second City. Before the days of urban renewal, Second City had been the neighborhood where black folk and day-workers employed by the prominent big houses on Queens Road lived and created a community of professional businesses— barbershops and beauty parlors, the original fast-food joints, and churches of every denomination on every corner, it seemed, and more. It was a prosperous neighborhood, thriving and happy with the smell of lilies blooming along the white picket fences, I'm told. This all ended with urban renewal when the city decided to relocate the neighborhood and develop the area so close to downtown into something more suitable and in line with modern society, something more fitting to be the backdrop of the up-and-coming skyline.

But I was new to Charlotte. I had no idea about where we were going and what to expect. I had rarely been out of eastern North Carolina. I had been to Greensboro and to the mountains once, but was sick most of the time because of a bad bus trip. As far as actually going west, the outskirts of Fayetteville had been it for me. I often wondered where that big west-bound highway stopped or if it just kept on rolling to the Pacific Ocean. All I knew was it was scary and dark, and I was always glad to get back to the safety of my home.

Well, by the time the moving truck was packed and the house was cleaned, it was late in the day when we started on our trip to Charlotte. A few neighbors came over with food and sandwiches they had prepared for us to take on the road for the children because we didn't know what would be open on the way.

The children were as excited as my husband and I were. The light in their eyes was amazing. They asked a million and one questions about where we were going. Famous last words were, "Are we there yet?"

Their father would answer gently, "It won't be long. Take a nap and I promise I will wake you when we get there." Well, I was like the children. I couldn't sleep. This was one of the first times I had been down Highway 74 past Fayetteville. We crossed bridges bigger than anything I remembered ever crossing. We stopped once to get peach ice cream from a little place beside the road. And one time we stopped at a huge truck stop just to stretch our legs and take a break. It seemed like this three-and-a-half-hour ride was taking forever. Some say that's because we didn't know where we were going, and the bigness of the place blew space and time out of proportion.

Finally, after passing all the cows and farmhouses and coming through the little towns of Wadesboro and Wingate, Monroe and Matthews, my husband said, "Wake up children, I want you to see this." I had drifted off to sleep myself and awoke to the happy chatter of my children asking, "Wow, Daddy, is this a foreign country?" Another child said, "I think us going to the Moon." Dee Dee, the oldest said, "Y'all being silly. That's the city."

I opened my eyes wide and from the hill in Matthews, we could see the skyline of Uptown Charlotte, looming like an island of lights. It did look like some faraway planet with tall buildings jutting upward like giants surrounded by a blue hue. My baby boy said, "Star Wars." We had just seen the first film in what would become a famous series, and the floating planets, all the stars, and the majesty of the movie, complete with the force, seemed to be manifesting themselves now right before our eyes.

I was in total awe as well. The fear that had been gripping my heart about the move to Charlotte was now replaced by anticipation and curiosity about what all those wonderful buildings held for me and my country-bumpkin children.

We drove into the city. More car lots than the law should allow lined Independence Boulevard and the boys started claiming their cars from the backseat. Construction was all around . . . and has not stopped over these past thirty years. But that night, hanging out the windows of that big blue station wagon, I was glad that all the people had gone home and I could just take it all in. We were kindred spirits with the Jed Clampetts from *The Beverly Hillbillies,* just in a fancier automobile. My sophisticated husband proceeded to give us a tour of Uptown, and then we arrived at our first lodging place.

It was a happy time, and I smile when I think of all the growth and changes, both physically and culturally, we have seen in the city since then. But nothing could ever impress me more than when we first drove into the Queen City and made this place of grandeur and light our home forever, or at least a very long time.

ELISHA T. "MOTHER" MINTER is a writer, storyteller, and actress. She has appeared in such stage productions as *The Wiz, South Pacific,* and *Proposals* (for which she won Actress of the Year from *Creative Loafing Charlotte*). She made her film debut in 2007 in *The Ultimate Gift,* starring James Garner. Her work has been published in *Charlotte Pride, Charlotte* magazine, and *Black Child USA,* where she wrote the "Parenting Points" column. She is working on a book entitled *Children's Play Songs from the African American Experience: In the Tradition.*

Making It a Better Place

ROBERT INMAN

DORSEY BASCOMBE is a character in my novel *Old Dogs and Children*—
a businessman and mayor of his small Southern town in the early 1920s.
He says to his wife and young daughter, "When you choose a place, choose
to live in it, you take from it and then you give part of yourself back.
This happens to be a good place, but it can be better. And I aim to do what
I can."

I wrote that when I was anchoring the news on Charlotte's WBTV in
the early 1990s, and I believed then that what Dorsey said applied to the
community I saw around me. It still does. There were then, and are now,
a mighty good number of Charlotteans who see an obligation to give back
to the place where they live, and do so in myriad creative ways. Giving
back, paying civic rent, seems to have been a way of life in Charlotte for
a long time. It goes far beyond mere civic boosterism. Anybody can *say*
they live in a good place. What really matters, though, is working—like
Dorsey Bascombe—to make a good place better.

One area where it manifests itself in Charlotte is local government.
My job as a journalist was partly to ask tough, impertinent questions of the
local officials I covered: to make sure that our viewers got a fair, impartial,

balanced view of their community, the issues that counted, and the people who led it. To ensure that citizens understood the stakes and that leaders were held accountable for what they did and said. My job was made considerably easier by the fact that I found a lot of good people in leadership positions: the city council, the county commission, the school board, business organizations, civic and cultural groups. They were overwhelmingly honest, motivated by a healthy mix of both self-interest and a sense of community responsibility.

Not that leadership was easy for those folks. My family and I arrived in Charlotte in 1970, the first year of court-ordered cross-town school bussing. There was a great deal of turmoil in the schools, a profound challenge to those of us in the news business to cover the story without exacerbating it. The school board was rife with factions: those who welcomed such a massive effort to integrate, those who were staunchly opposed, those who occupied a middle ground. But with the wise, firm leadership of chairman Bill Poe, the board finally came to a conclusion: *Whether we like this or not, the kids matter the most, and we have to make it work.* And they did, accommodating across ideological fault lines to make their community better.

It was the guiding principle for other governing bodies. The late Stan Brookshire told me once about how a delegation of local leaders came to him and urged him to run for mayor. Mr. Brookshire was a successful businessman, actively involved in many areas of civic life, a moderate consensus-builder. "I'll run," he told the delegation, "but I want you to know that if I'm elected, I won't be beholden to you fellows, only to what's best for Charlotte." The delegates said, in effect, "that's exactly why we want you to run." He did, and won, and led Charlotte through the touchy civil rights era of the 1960s when other Southern cities were wracked by violence. Charlotte, with the guidance of Stan Brookshire and like-minded people, simply did the right thing, and made their community a better place for the doing.

Business leaders like Stan Brookshire and those who came before and after have generally had the attitude that a solid community with a sense of moral responsibility is good for business. And the success of the business community bears that out. Charlotte is an economic engine of considerable proportions, a booming center of finance, distribution, retail, manufacturing, service. Lots of good jobs. But jobs belong to people, and business leaders have contributed mightily to those things that make the city a good place to live, and have only tangential relationship to commerce. They've helped make it a place that attracts good people from all over the world to fill jobs. And as new people arrive, they've tried to pass along the legacy of volunteerism, involvement, caring.

I thought about Stan Brookshire and the legions of other good Charlotte people as I sat at the annual holiday season gathering of the Goodfellows. Almost fifteen-hundred men packed a ballroom at the convention center to raise about $400,000 to help Charlotte's working poor. The next day, more than a thousand women, members of the Good Friends and their guests, sat around the same ballroom tables and contributed more than $170,000 to the same cause. It's a tradition that goes back almost a hundred years. In the Goodfellows audience, I noted a preponderance of middle-aged and older folks, but also a large contingent of younger men. Many came as guests of the older crowd, who were saying, *This is how we do things in Charlotte. We're a compassionate community, and if you're going to live here, you have to give back.*

The Goodfellows and Good Friends are the norm, not the exception. The vehicles for compassionate service are legion: The Empty Stocking Fund, Crisis Assistance Ministry, United Way, civic clubs, religious organizations—the list covers pages and the record of good done in and by the community fills volumes. Some years ago, one of our news stories was about the homeless shelter, how it was being almost overwhelmed with people who had no place to go. The word had gotten out across the country that Charlotte had a vigorous, generous attitude toward the homeless, and they flocked to the city in droves. Somehow, Charlotte managed to take them in and give them a hand. It was another instance where good people did good things and added to the tradition.

Charlotte is a go-go community these days: dynamic, exciting, vigorous, going places. It's a melting pot of people and cultures from all over the world, more on the way. It's a good place to work, live, worship, thrive, grow, make friends, raise a family. I like to think, after investing forty-plus years of my life in Charlotte, that it's a special place, unique among America's urban areas. The future looks profoundly bright. But what will keep it special and unique has a lot to do with its roots in the past, the tradition of good people seeing that a good place can always be made better, and acting on it. Dorsey Bascombe would be proud.

ROBERT INMAN is the author of five novels—*Home Fires Burning, Old Dogs and Children, Dairy Queen Days, Captain Saturday,* and his latest, *The Governor's Lady*. He has written screenplays for six motion pictures for television, including two Hallmark Hall of Fame Productions, and seven produced and published stage plays. From 1970–96 he was principal news anchor for Charlotte's WBTV.

About the Cover

The cover illustration for 27 *Views of Charlotte* is the work of Chapel Hill writer and artist Daniel Wallace. His illustrations appear in many publications, including the *Los Angeles Times, Italian Vanity Fair,* and *Our State Magazine.* He illustrated the book covers of 27 *Views of Hillsborough,* 27 *Views of Chapel Hill,* 27 *Views of Asheville,* 27 *Views of Durham,* and 27 *Views of Raleigh,* all published by Eno Publishers. He also illustrated *Papadaddy's Book for New Fathers,* by Clyde Edgerton.

Award-winning Books from Eno Publishers

27 Views of Raleigh
The City of Oaks in Prose & Poetry
INTRODUCTION BY WILTON BARNHARDT
$15.95/224 pages

27 Views of Durham
The Bull City in Prose & Poetry
INTRODUCTION BY STEVE SCHEWEL
$15.95/216 pages

27 Views of Asheville
A Southern Mountain Town in Prose & Poetry
INTRODUCTION BY ROB NEUFELD
$15.95/216 pages

27 Views of Chapel Hill
A Southern University Town in Prose & Poetry
INTRODUCTION BY DANIEL WALLACE
$16.50/240 pages

27 Views of Hillsborough
A Southern Town in Prose & Poetry
INTRODUCTION BY MICHAEL MALONE
$15.95/216 pages
Gold IPPY Book Award, Best Anthology
Gold Eric Hoffer Book Award, Culture

Eno's books are available at your local bookshop and from www.enopublishers.org

Chapel Hill in Plain Sight
Notes from the Other Side of the Tracks
DAPHNE ATHAS
$16.95/246 pages

Undaunted Heart
The True Story of a Southern Belle & a Yankee General
SUZY BARILE
$16.95/238 pages
Silver IPPY Book Award, Best Regional Nonfiction

Brook Trout & the Writing Life
The Intermingling of Fishing & Writing in a Novelist's Life
CRAIG NOVA
$15.95/152 pages

Rain Gardening in the South
Ecologically Designed Gardens for Drought,
Deluge & Everything in Between
HELEN KRAUS & ANNE SPAFFORD
$19.95/144 pages
Gold Book Award, Garden Writers Association
Silver Book Award, Garden Writers Association
Silver Benjamin Franklin Book Award
Honorable Mention, Eric Hoffer Book Award